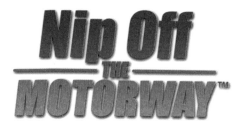

..for thousands of places to eat, drink, sleep, shop and more.

Published by MK Publishing Ltd.
2004

Published by MK Publishing Ltd.
Wheatsheaf House, Montgomery Street
East Kilbride G74 4JS
Tel: 01355 222400   Fax: 01355 245064
E-mail: contact@nipoffthemotorway.co.uk
Web: www.nipoffthemotorway.co.uk

ISBN 0-9548547-0-5

Nip Off The Motorway

WELCOME to Nip Off The Motorway – your passport to thousands of off-motorway facilities within easy reach of motorway exits.

As you drive on Britain's motorways you can use this book to find the nearest junction that has just what you want - whether that is a cup of tea in a quiet garden centre, a steak supper in a pub restaurant, a bed for the night or just a walk in the park.

We have made Nip Off The Motorway very user-friendly so you will have no trouble in finding your way around it. The summary pages list the junctions in order along a particular motorway, showing in symbol format what is available at each junction and giving you the appropriate page number to turn to.
On the junction detail page you will find a clear OS™ map positioning each place that is available at that junction plus a list of these places with their postcode, a contact phone number and simple directions.

Symbols

	Hotel or B&B		Children's play area
	Petrol	£	Cash point
	Food		Shops
	Alcoholic drinks	HGV	Parking suitable for HGV's
	Soft / Hot drinks		Swimming pool
	Car repairs/spares		No smoking area
(TTD)	Things to do	PICNIC/ PARK	Designated areas shown on maps
	Wheelchair access		

Happy Travelling!

Contents

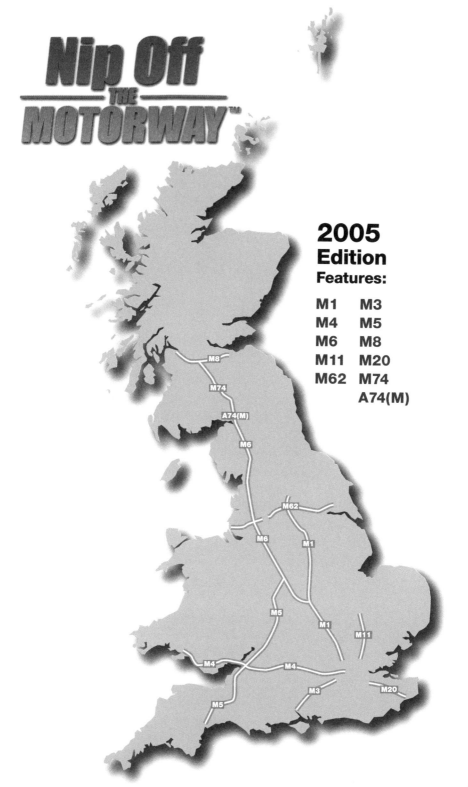

Nip Off THE MOTORWAY™

2005
Edition
Features:

M1	M3
M4	M5
M6	M8
M11	M20
M62	M74
	A74(M)

🛏️☕✕🍴 **16**	**Northampton A45**	*Page 12*
	4 miles	
⛽🛒 **15a**	**Oxford A43**	*Page 11*
	(Rothersthorpe Services)	
	3 miles	
🛏️☕✕✎ TTD 🍴 **15**	**Northampton A508**	*Page 11*
	9 miles	
●	**Newport Pagnell Services**	
	3 miles	
🛏️☕✕✎⛽🍴 **14**	**Newport Pagnell A509**	*Page 10*
	5 miles	
🛏️☕✕ TTD 🍴 **13**	**Milton Keynes A421**	*Page 10*
	7 miles	
🛏️☕✕✎⛽ TTD 🍴 **12**	**Flitwick A5120**	*Page 9*
	1 mile	
●	**Toddington Services**	
	4 miles	
🛏️☕✕✎⛽🛒🏊🍴 **11**	**Dunstable A505**	*Page 9*
	3 miles	
☕✕⛽ TTD 🍴 **10**	**Luton A1081**	*Page 8*
	2 miles	
🛏️☕✕⛽ TTD 🍴 **9**	**Harpenden A5**	*Page 8*
	5 miles	
🛏️☕✕✎⛽🛒🍴 **8**	**Hemel Hempstead A414**	*Page 7*
	1 mile	
No Accessible Facilities **7**	**M10**	
	2 miles	
No Accessible Facilities **6a**	**M25**	
	1 mile	
[M] 🛏️☕✕⛽🍴 **6**	**St Albans A405**	*Page 7*
	2 miles	
🛏️☕✕✎ TTD 🛒🍴 **5**	**Watford A41**	*Page 6*
	4 miles	
No Accessible Facilities **4**	**Edgware A41**	
	1 mile	
●	**London Gateway Services**	
	3 miles	
No Accessible Facilities **2**	**The City A1**	
	2 miles	
[M] 🛏️☕✕✎⛽🛒🍴 **1**	**London A406**	*Page 6*
	Total Dist. = 62 miles	

NORTH ⬆️

		Location	Page
🛏️☕✕⛽🍴	29	**Mansfield, Chesterfield A617**	*Page 17*
		4 miles	
	●	**Tibshelf Services**	
		3 miles	
🛏️☕✕🍴	28	**Mansfield A38**	*Page 17*
		4 miles	
⛽🛒	27	**Hucknall A608**	*Page 16*
		6 miles	
☕✕🍴	26	**Ilkeston A610**	*Page 16*
		3 miles	
	●	**Trowell Services**	
		3 miles	
🛏️☕✕✂️⛽	25	**Nottingham A52**	*Page 15*
		4 miles	
No Accessible Facilities	24a	**Derby A50**	
		1 mile	
🛏️☕✕⛽🍴	24	**Uttoxeter A50, A453** (Donington Park Services)	*Page 15*
		2 miles	
No Accessible Facilities	23a	**Birmingham A42**	
		5 miles	
🛏️☕✕✂️(TTD)	23	**Loughborough A512**	*Page 14*
		5 miles	
🛏️☕✕⛽🛒🍴	22	**Ashby A511, A50**	*Page 14*
		6 miles	
No Accessible Facilities	21a	**Leicester A46**	
		2 miles	
	●	**Leicester Forest East Services**	
		1 mile	
M ASDA 🛏️☕✕✂️⛽🛒	21	**Leicester A5460, M69**	*Page 13*
		11 miles	
🛏️☕✕✂️🛒🍴	20	**Lutterworth A4303, A4304**	*Page 13*
		3 miles	
No Accessible Facilities	19	**Kettering A14, M6**	
		4 miles	
🛏️☕✕⛽🍴	18	**Rugby A428**	*Page 12*
		2 miles	
No Accessible Facilities	17	**M45**	
		2 miles	
	●	**Watford Gap Services**	
		6 miles	
🛏️☕✕🍴	16	**Northampton A45**	*Page 12*
		Total Dist. = 77 miles	

4

🛏🍺✕(TTD)🛒🍷 **47** **Garforth A642** .... *Page 25*

3 miles

🅼 🛏🍺✕⛽(TTD)🛒🍷 **46** **Leeds A6120, A63** .... *Page 24*

4 miles

🍺✕🔧(TTD)🛒 **45** **Leeds** .... *Page 24*

4 miles

🅼 *Kwik-Fit* 🛏🍺✕🔧⛽🛒🍷 **44** **Leeds A639** .... *Page 23*

1 mile

No Accessible Facilities **42/43** **M62/M621**

3 miles

🛏🍺✕🔧⛽🛒🍷 **41** **Morley A650** .... *Page 23*

3 miles

🅼 🛏🍺✕🛒🍷 **40** **Wakefield, Dewsbury A638** . *Page 22*

3 miles

🛏🍺✕🔧⛽(TTD)🛒🍷 **39** **Wakefield A636** .... *Page 22*

2 miles

Woolley Edge Services

1 mile

🛏🍺✕(TTD)🍷 **38** **Huddersfield A637** .... *Page 21*

5 miles

Kwik-Fit 🛏🍺✕🔧⛽🍷 **37** **Barnsley A628** .... *Page 21*

4 miles

🅼 🛏🍺✕🔧⛽(TTD)🛒🍷 **36** **Sheffield A61** .... *Page 20*

2 miles

No Accessible Facilities **35a** **Stocksbridge A616**

2 miles

ASDA 🛏🍺✕🔧⛽🛒🍷 **35** **Rotherham A629** .... *Page 20*

3 miles

🅼 **Meadowhall** 🛏🍺✕🔧⛽🛒🍷 **34** **Sheffield A6109** .... *Page 19*

3 miles

halfords 🛏🍺✕🔧⛽🏊🍷 **33** **Rotherham, Sheffield A630** . *Page 19*

3 miles

No Accessible Facilities **32** **M18**

2 miles

🛏🍺✕⛽🛒🍷 **31** **Worksop, Sheffield A57** .... *Page 18*

3 miles

Woodall Services

2 miles

🅼 🛏🍺✕⛽(TTD)🛒🍷 **30** **Sheffield A6135, A619** .... *Page 18*

7 miles

🛏🍺✕⛽🍷 **29** **Mansfield, Chesterfield, A619** *Page 18*

Total Dist. = 60 miles

NORTH

M1 Jn 1

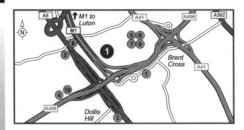

1. Holiday Inn NW2 1LP ♿
   Tel: 0870 400 9112
   Bear right under bridge, 1st left, on right

2. Victoria Filling Station NW2 6LH
   Tel: 020 84503697
   Right A406, left A5, on right

3. National Tyres And Autocare NW9 7BN
   Tel: 020 82020161
   Right A406, right A5, on left

4. Partco NW2 7AQ
   Tel: 020 82082025
   Right A406, on right

5. Burger King NW4 3FZ
   Tel: 020 82025955
   In Brent Cross Shopping Centre

6.		**MCDONALD'S RESTAURANT NW4 3FQ** Tel: 020 82038412	⬛🏫♿ ✗🚭
		In Brent Cross Shopping Centre	

7. Pizza Hut NW4 3FZ
   In Brent Cross Shopping Centre

8. Mehfil Indian Restaurant NW4 3PQ
   Right A406, right A5, on right

9. Waitrose Supermarket NW4 3FQ
   In Brent Cross Shopping Centre

10. Shell Petrol Station NW11 9BY
    Left A406, right A502, on right

M1 Jn 5

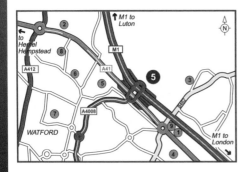

1. Hilton Hotel WD25 8HA
   Tel: 01923 235881
   A41 South, on left

2. Sainsburys Supermarket WD25 9JS
   Tel: 01923 680978
   A41 North, on right

3. Aldenham Golf & Country Club WD25 8NN
   Tel: 01923 853929
   A41 South, left B462, on left

4. Quincey's American Restaurant WD25 8HH
   Tel: 01923 229137
   A41 South, on right

5. Top Golf Game Centre WD24 7AB
   Tel: 01923 222045
   At r'bout Berry Gr ln, rt to Bushey Ml Ln, on rt

6. Tudor Arms Pub Restaurant WD24 7TQ
   Tel: 01923 225105
   At r'bout Berry Gr ln, rt to Bushey Ml Ln, on rt

7. HI-Q Tyre Services WD24 4YY
   Tel: 01923 246864
   A4008 South, rt at two r'bouts, 1st left, on left

8. Partco Autoparts Ltd WD24 7GP
   Tel: 01923 225978
   A41 North, lt W/mere Av, rt B/Mill Ln, rt G/cain Rd

9. Toby Carvery (Oldenham) WD25 8AB
   A41 South, on left

M1 Jn 6

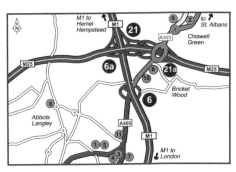

1. Frankie & Bennys WD25 7JZ
Tel: 01923 662690
A405 South

2. Little Chef AL2 2AB
Tel: 01727 839998
A405 North

3. **MCDONALD'S RESTAURANT WD25 0NH**
Tel: 01923 671550
A405 South

4. TGI Fridays WD25 0LH
Tel: 01923 672310
A405 South, left fork

5. Chiquito Mexican Restaurant WD25 7JZ
Tel: 01923 682321
A405 South

6. Classic Petrol Station AL2 3RS
Tel: 01923 680024
A405 North, on right

7. Orchard House Guest House WD25 9QJ
Tel: 01923 672376
A405 South, left fork

8. The Compasses Hotel & Restaurant WD5 0LJ
Tel: 01923 262870
A405 South, right to Horseshoe Lane

9. The Thistle Hotel AL2 3DS
Tel: 01727 854252
A405 North

10. **THE VICEROY OF INDIA AL2 3UN**
Tel: 01923 672121
Award Winning Restaurant, est. since 1991
A405 North

11. Three Horseshoes Restaurant WD25 0LL
Tel: 01923 678027
A405 South

M1 Jn 8

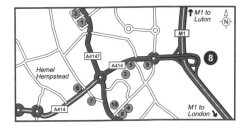

1. Nationwide Autocentres HP2 7BW
Tel: 01442 245634
A414 West, A4147 North, on left

2. Rac Auto Windscreens HP2 7BH
Tel: 01442 242322
A414 West, A4147 North, on left

3. Shell Petrol Station HP2 4TZ
Tel: 01442 275010
A414 West

4. Spar HP3 8QG
Tel: 01442 213060
A414 West, left at 2nd r'bout, on left

5. Holiday Inn HP2 4UA
Tel: 0870 400 9041
A414 West

6. The Hawthorns Guest House HP2 4HJ
Tel: 01442 213250
After 2 r'bouts, 1st right

7. The Plough Restaurant HP3 8PR
Tel: 01442 213881
A414 West, 1st left after 2nd r'bout

8. Three Horseshoes Filling Station HP3 8QE
Tel: 01442 268390
A414 West, left at 2nd r'bout

9. BP Petrol Station HP2 4TZ
Tel: 01442 269003
A414 West

10. Elite Windscreens HP2 4NZ
Tel: 01442 235859
A414 West, left at 2nd r'bout

M1 Jn 9

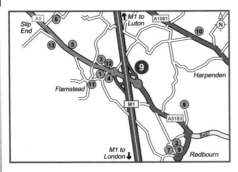

1. Express By Holiday Inn AL3 8HT &
   Tel: 01582 841332
   A5 towards Dunstable next to Harvester

2. Country House Restaurant AL3 7LW
   Tel: 01582 792756
   A5183, fork right

3. Flamstead Filling Station AL3 8HS
   Tel: 01582 842098
   A5 North

4. Harvester Restaurant AL3 8HT
   Tel: 01582 842800
   A5 North

5. Hertfordshire Moat House AL3 8HH
   Tel: 01582 449988
   A5 North

6. High Winds Farm Guest House AL3 8LW
   Tel: 01582 841198
   A5 North, right Hicks Rd

7. Indian Nights Restaurant AL3 7LN
   Tel: 01582 794119
   A5183, fork right

8. Redbourn Golf Club AL3 7QA
   Tel: 01582 793493
   A5183, left Luton Ln

9. The Bull Inn AL3 7LW &
   Tel: 01582 792392
   A5183 St Albans, right 2nd r'bout

10. The Peppercorn Restaurant AL5 3NG
    Tel: 01582 713891
    A5183 , left Luton Ln, right The Common

11. The Three Blackbirds (Pub Restaurant) AL3 8BS
    Tel: 01582 840330
    A5 North, left to Flamstead

12. Watling Street Filling Station AL3 8HA
    Tel: 01582 840215
    A5 North

13. Mela Indian Restaurant AL3 8JP
    A5 North

M1 Jn 10

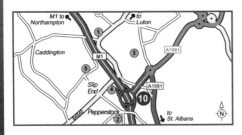

1. Farley Green Service Station LU1 5QA
   Tel: 01582 407032
   Right at r'bout, 1st right, on B4540

2. Halfmoon Restaurant LU1 4LL
   Tel: 01582 722964
   Right at r'bout, 2nd right, left Halfmoon Lane

3. Stockwood Park Golf Club LU1 4LX
   Tel: 01582 413704
   Left at r'bout

4. The Frog & Rhubarb (Pub Restaurant) LU1 4BJ
   Tel: 01582 452722
   Right at r'bout, 1st right, 1st left

5. The Plough (Pub Restaurant) LU1 4LU
   Tel: 01582 720923
   Right at r'bout, 2nd rt, over B4540, rt at T-junc

M1 Jn 11

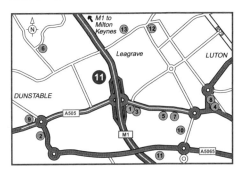

1. Fuelforce LU4 8QR
   Tel: 01582 574366
   At East side of junction

2. Tesco Supermarket LU5 4JU
   Tel: 0845 677 9226
   A505 West, left at r'bout, on right

3. Travelodge LU4 8RQ
   Tel: 01582 575955
   At East side of junction

4. Empire Service Station LU4 8DL
   Tel: 01582 593886
   A505 East, on left

5. Leicester Arms Restaurant LU4 8QW
   Tel: 01582 572718
   A505 East, on right

6. Lewsey Park Swimming Pool LU4 0PF
   Tel: 01582 604244
   A505 West, rt Lewsey Rd, lt L/grave Hi St, rt Pastures Wy

7. Sunview Guest House LU4 8QN
   Tel: 01582 491870
   A505 East, on right

8. The Chiltern Hotel LU4 9RU
   Tel: 01582 575911
   A505 East, left to Waller Ave

9. Travel Inn & Beefeater LU5 4LL
   Tel: 0870 19770873
   A505 West, on right over r'bout

10. Autoglass LU4 8EZ
    Tel: 01582 504590
    A505 East, right at r'bout, on right

11. Partco LU1 1XL
    Tel: 01582 402722
    A505 East, right at 2 r'bout, on left

12. Ats Euromaster LU4 9JU
    Tel: 01582 507020
    A505 East, 1st left, left at r'bout, on right

13. Kingfisher Petrol Station LU4 9LQ
    Tel: 01582 571791
    A505 East, 1st left, left at r'bout, left at T-junc

M1 Jn 12

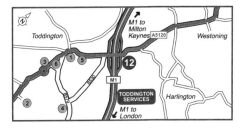

1. Bombay Tandoori Restaurant LU5 6BP
   Tel: 01525 874918
   A5120 South, on left

2. Chalgrave Manor Golf Club LU5 6JN
   Tel: 01525 876556
   A5120 South, on left

3. Norbury Hill Service Station LU5 6DR
   Tel: 01525 875420
   A5120 South, on right

4. The Fancott Pub Restaurant LU5 6HT
   Tel: 01525 872366
   A5120 South, left B530, in Fancott

5. The Griffin Hotel LU5 6BN
   Tel: 01525 872030
   A5120 South, on left

6. A J Autos Windscreens LU5 6BX
   Tel: 01525 877826
   A5120 South, on left

M1 Jn 13

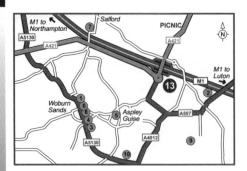

1. Harry Ramsdens MK17 8RX
Tel: 01908 583144
A4012, right A5130

2. Firs Guest House MK43 0TY
Tel: 01525 280279
A507 Ridgmont, on left through village

3. Firtree Hotel MK17 8SY
Tel: 01908 582127
A4012, right A5130

4. Jalori Indian Cuisine MK17 8RF
Tel: 01908 281239
A4012, right A5130

5. Moore Place Hotel MK17 8DW
Tel: 01908 282000
Turn right to Aspley Guise

6. Spooners Restaurant MK17 8QY
Tel: 01908 584385
A4012, right A5130

7. The Red Lion (Hotel) MK17 8AZ
Tel: 01908 583117
A421 West, right Wavendon Rd

8. The Woburn Fort (Indian Restaurant) MK17 8RB
Tel: 01908 282002
A4012, right A5130

9. Woburn Safari Park MK17 9QN
Tel: 01525 290407
Singposted from junction

10. The Birch Restaurant MK17 9HX
A4012, right A5130

M1 Jn 14

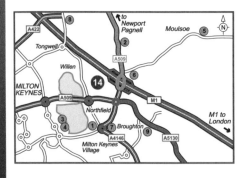

1. Express By Holiday Inn MK15 0YA
Tel: 01908 681000
A4146 south, at 2nd r'bout

2. The Courtyard By Marriott Milton Keynes MK16 0JA
Tel: 01908 613688
A509 north, on right.

3. Travel Inn MK15 9HQ
Tel: 0870 197 7185
A509 Milton Keynes, left at 2nd r'bout, on left.

4. Lakeside 241 (Restaurant) MK15 9HQ
Tel: 01908 675222
A509 Milton Keynes, left at 2nd r'bout, on left.

5. The Carrington Arms MK16 0HB
Tel: 01908 218050
A509 Newport Pagnell, 1st right

6. The Old Stables (Guest House) MK16 0HR
Tel: 01908 217766
A509 north, 1st right, 1st right

7. Total Filling Station MK10 9AB
Tel: 01908 559340
A4146 south, at r'bout

8. Clays Vehicle Repairs MK16 0JJ
Tel: 01908 616158
A509 south, rt at 3 r'bouts, on right

9. Sinton Tyres Ltd MK16 0HF
Tel: 01908 665591
A5130, on right

M1 Jn 15

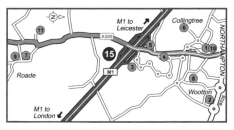

1. Burger King NN4 0JN
   Tel: 01604 701078
   A508 North, on left

2. Wootton Tyre & Exhaust Centre NN4 6HN
   Tel: 01604 660644
   A508 North, right B526, right at r'bout, on left

3. Express By Holiday Inn NN4 5FB
   Tel: 01604 432800
   At Junction

4. Little Chef NN4 0LY
   Tel: 01604 705722
   A508 North, on right

5. The Hilton NN4 0XW
   Tel: 01604 700666
   A508 North, on left

6. Collingtree Park Golf Course NN4 0XN
   Tel: 01604 700000
   A508 North, left Rowntree Rd, left Winding Brook Ln

7. Roade House Hotel NN7 2NW
   Tel: 01604 863372
   A508 South, 2 miles from junction ♿

8. Stanstead Hotels NN4 6EY
   Tel: 01604 661791
   A508 North, cross A508 to Wootton, on left

9. The Cock At Roade (Pub Restaurant) NN7 2NW
   Tel: 01604 862544
   A508 South, left High St Roade, on right

10. The Toby Carvery & Innkeepers Lodge NN4 0TG
    Tel: 01604 769676
    A508 North, on left

11. Homech Auto Services NN7 2PT
    Tel: 01604 863250
    A508 South, right Bailey Brook Lane

M1 Jn 15a

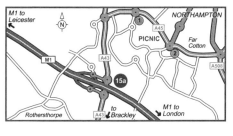

1. The Hill Shop Supermarket NN4 9UW
   Tel: 01604 767108
   A43 North, A45 East, right at 1st r'bout

2. Tesco Supermarket & Petrol NN4 0JF
   A43 North, A45 East, at 2nd r'bout

M1 Jn 16

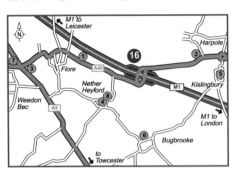

3. Crossroads Premier Lodge NN7 4PX
   Tel: 0870 990 6364
   A45 West, at junction with A5

4. The Forester's Arms Pub & B+B NN7 3LE
   Tel: 01327 340622
   A45 West, left Nether Heyford

5. The Olde Red Lion NN7 4AQ   ♿
   Tel: 01604 830219
   A45 Northampton, right at r'bout, in village on right

6. The Five Bells Bugbrooke NN7 3PB
   Tel: 01604 832483
   A45 Northampton, right at r'bout   ♿

7. The Globe Hotel NN7 4QD
   Tel: 01327 340336
   A45 Weedon Beck, after A5

8. The Olde Sun NN7 3LL
   Tel: 01327 340164
   A45 Daventry, left to Nether Heyford

1. Courtyard By Marriott Daventry Hotel NN7 4LP
   Tel: 01327 349022
   A45 Daventry, on right   ♿

2. Travel Inn & Beefeater NN7 4DD
   Tel: 0870 197 7195
   A45 East, on left

M1 Jn 18

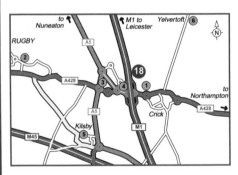

3. Halfway Garage CV23 8YE
   Tel: 01788 822614
   A428 Rugby. On 3rd roundabout

4. Ibis Hotel NN6 7EX
   Tel: 01788 824331
   A428 Rugby, on right

5. The Hunt House Restaurant CV23 8XR
   Tel: 01788 823282
   A5 South, right to Kilsby, left Main Rd

6. The Knightley Arms (Pub with food) NN6 6LF
   Tel: 01788 822401
   A428 N/ampton, left to Yelvertoft, right   ♿

1. The Holiday Inn NN6 7XR
   Tel: 01788 824800
   A428 East, on left

2. Exotica Bengal Cuisine CV21 4NU
   Tel: 01788 547187
   A428 Rugby, rt to Watts Ln, rt   ♿

M1 Jn 20

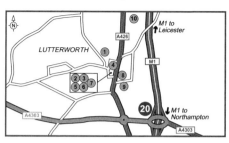

5. Paper Tiger Chinese Restaurant LE17 4AE
Tel: 01455 552365
On A426 North

6. Pizzaman LE17 4AW
Tel: 01455 553100
A4303 Lutterworth, left to Church St

7. **THE GREYHOUND COACHING INN LE17 4EJ**
Tel: 01455 553307
Family run, 32 e/s beds, fresh prep food
Main road through Lutterworth, top of hill

1. Safeway Supermarket LE17 4EZ
Tel: 01455 550223
A426 North, left Church St, right Bitteswell Rd

2. Cheikos Restaurant LE17 4AW
Tel: 01455 559869
On A426 North

3. Exotic Spice Indian Restaurant LE17 4AE
Tel: 01455 203000
A426 Lutterworth, on left

4. Co-Op Supermarket LE17 4EE
Tel: 01455 557225
On A426 North

8. The Shambles Inn LE17 4DW
Tel: 01455 552620
On A426 North

9. Lutterworth Motor Spares LE17 4AP
Tel: 01455 557336
On Lutterworth High St, right at top, 50 yds on rt

10. Steer Tyres Ltd LE17 4HD
Tel: 01455 553666
A426 North, on right

M1 Jn 21

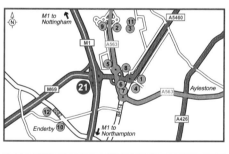

1. **ASDA LEICESTER LE3 2LL**
Tel: 0116 281 5000
Straight over r'bout

2. Burger King LE19 1JZ
Tel: 0116 289 3884
A563 North, in Braunstone

3. Frankie & Bennys LE19 1JZ
Tel: 0116 282 4254
A563 North, in Braunstone

4. **MCDONALD'S RESTAURANT LE19 1HX**
Tel: 0116 263 0563
Right at r'bout

5. **MCDONALD'S RESTAURANT LE19 2WZ**
Tel: 0116 282 5700
A563 North, off on left

6. Pizza Hut LE19 1WW
Tel: 0116 289 2990
Straight ahead, on right

7. Sainsburys Supermarket LE19 1WT
Tel: 0116 263 1153
Straight ahead, on right

8. The Hilton Leicester LE19 1WQ
Tel: 0116 263 0066
Straight ahead, on left

9. Travel Inn LE19 1LU
Tel: 0870 197 7154
A563 North, off to left

10. C I N I Restaurant LE19 4AG
Tel: 0116 286 3009
B4114 South, 1st right, in Enderby

11. Chiquito Mexican Restaurant LE19 1JZ
Tel: 0116 289 4141
A563 North, in Braunstone

12. Autoglass LE19 4AV
Tel: 0116 284 8585
B4114 South, 1st right

M1 Jn 22

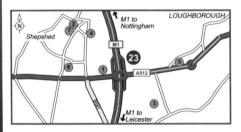

1. Abbots Oak Country House Hotel LE67 4UY
Tel: 01530 832328
B591 North, left at lights, on left

2. The Birch Tree LE67 1TD
Tel: 01530 832134
A511 West

3. BP Petrol Station LE67 9PU
Tel: 01530 249849
A511 West, at r'bout

4. Charnwood Arms Hotel LE67 1TB
Tel: 01530 813644
A511 West, left at 2nd r'bout

5. Field Head Hotel LE67 9PS
Tel: 01530 245454
A50 East, left at r'bout

6. Co-Op Supermarket LE67 9TN
Tel: 01530 242213
A511 West, left to Stanton under Barton

7. Total Petrol Station LE67 4BL
Tel: 01530 811172
A511 West

8. Travelodge LE67 9PP
Tel: 0870 0850950
West of junction

M1 Jn 23

1. Junction 23 Lorry Park & Café LE12 9BS
Tel: 01509 507480
On A512 West

2. Kims Café LE12 9QE
Tel: 01509 502286
A512 West, right Charnwood Rd

3. Longcliffe Golf Club LE11 3YA
Tel: 01509 239129
A512 East, right Snell's Nook Lane

4. The Grange Courtyard (Guest House) LE12 9DA
Tel: 01509 600189
A512 West, right Leicester Rd, in Forest St

5. The Quality Hotel LE11 4EX
Tel: 01509 211800
A512 East, on left

6. Tyrex LE12 9NJ
Tel: 01509 508001
A512 West, right Charnwood Rd, right Old Station Close

7. Yam Sing Inn (Chinese Restaurant) LE12 9QE
Tel: 01509 650066
A512 West, right Charnwood Rd

M1 Jn 24

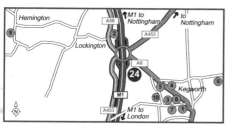

1. Ye Olde Flying Horse DE74 2ED
Tel: 01509 672253
A6 Loughborough, on right

2. Hilton DE74 2YW
Tel: 01509 674000
Take A50 North, on right

3. Kegworth House Guest House DE74 2DA
Tel: 01509 672575
A6 Kegworth, rt to High Street

4. Kegworth Service Station DE74 2EN
Tel: 01509 673435
A6 Kegworth.

5. Kegworth Whitehouse Hotel DE74 2DF
Tel: 01509 672427
A6 to Loughborough, 500 yards on right. 1st right for car park.

6. The Anchor Inn DE74 2FR
Tel: 01509 672722
A5 Kegworth, 1st left, on right

7. The Coach House DE74 2DA
Tel: 01509 674131
A6 Kegworth, rt to High Street

8. The Cottage Restaurant DE74 2DA
Tel: 01509 672449
A6 Kegworth, rt to High Street

9. The Jolly Sailor DE74 2RB
Tel: 01332 810448
Denby A50, lt Lockington, lt to Hemington, lt at Main St.

10. Yew Lodge Hotel DE74 2DF
Tel: 01509 672518
A6 Kegworth, 1st right, on right

M1 Jn 25

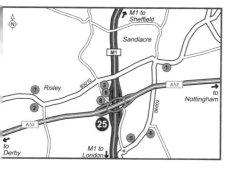

1. Autoglass NG10 5AH
Tel: 0115 949 1944
At r'bout take Bostocks Ln (N), rt to Derby Rd, on rt

2. Braeside Guest House DE72 3SS
Tel: 0115 939 5885
Risley exit, left, on left

3. Branaghan's Restaurant NG10 5NL
Tel: 0115 946 2000
At r'bout take Bostocks lane (N), on right

4. Longmoor Road Service Station NG10 4FN
Tel: 0115 946 5849
At r'bout take Bostocks Lane (S), lt at r'bout, on rt

5. Novotel NG10 4EP
Tel: 0115 946 5111
At r'bout take Bostocks Lane (S), on left.

6. Ramada Hotel NG10 5NL
Tel: 0115 946 0000
At r'bout take Bostocks Lane (N), on right.

7. Risley Hall Hotel Ltd DE72 3SS
Tel: 0115 939 9000
At r'bout take Bostocks Lane (N), lt at X-roads, on rt

8. Holiday Inn NG10 5NJ
Tel: 0870 4009062
At r'bout take Bostocks Lane (N), on right.

M1 Jn 26

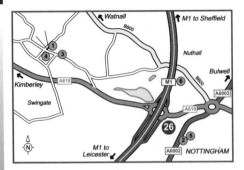

1. Dillingers Bar & Diner NG16 2NG
Tel: 0115 938 4664
A610 Nottingham, left B600, on right

2. Brewsters NG16 1QE
Tel: 0115 976 2200
A610 Nottingham, right A6002, on left

3. Sainsburys Supermarket NG16 2LY
Tel: 0115 938 2046
A610 Nottingham, left B600, on left

4. Simla Tandoori Restaurant NG16 2LP
Tel: 0115 945 9350
A610 Nottingham, left B600, on left

5. Sinatras Restaurant (Italian, Spanish and Mexican) NG16 1PT
Tel: 0115 975 0005
A610 Nottingham, right A6002, left at Brewsters, next to Spar

6. The Laziza Indian Restaurant NG16 1DP
A610 Nottingham, left B600, on left

M1 Jn 27

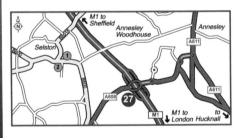

1. Somerfield Supermarket NG16 6BT
Tel: 01773 861643
A608 South, B600, on right

2. Green Service Station NG16 6BX
A608 South, B600, on left

M1 Jn 28

1. Burger King DE55 2ER
Tel: 01773 545270
On B6019

2. Co-op Supermarket DE55 2BN
Tel: 01773 583472
B6019, right Market Street

3. Hawthorne Carvery & Bars DE55 2AS
Tel: 01773 811328
On B6019

4. PIT STOP CAFE & SANDWICH BAR DE55 2DY
Tel: 01773 580480
Hot & cold food to eat in or take away
A38 North, 1st left, 1st right, on left

5. RENAISSANCE DERBY/NOTTINGHAM HOTEL
Tel: 01773 812000   **DE55 2EH**
Costa Coffee, great menu choice, 158 rooms
A38 North, 1st left

6. Brewers Fayre DE55 2EH
Tel: 0870 197 7180
A38 North, 1st left

7. Spud-U-Like DE55 2ER
On B6019

M1 Jn 29

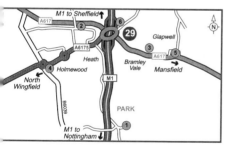

1. HARDWICK INN COUNTRY PUB S44 5QJ
Tel: 01246 850245
Fresh home cooked food all day every day
A6175, 1st left, follow green signs

2. Heath Service Station S44 5SF
Tel: 01246 850525
A617 West

3. Ma Hubbard's Restaurant S44 5LY
Tel: 01246 857236
A617 East

4. The Jolly Farmer S42 5RB
Tel: 01246 855608
A6175 West

5. The Young Vanish (Public House) S44 5NB
Tel: 01623 810238
A617 East

6. Twin Oaks Motel S44 6UZ
Tel: 01246 855455
At junction

M1 Jn 30

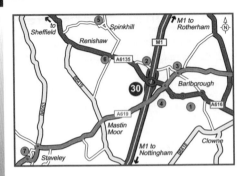

1. **Barlborough Links Golf Club S43 4WN**
   Tel: 01246 813111
   A616, after half mile

2. **Dusty Miller (Pub Restaurant) S43 4TW**
   Tel: 01246 810507
   A6135, right

3. **Widdowson B & B S43 4ER**
   Tel: 01246 810974
   East from junction, left at 2 r'bouts

4. **McDonalds Restaurant S43 4WP**
   Tel: 01246 819520
   A616 east, right at r'bout

5. **The Angel Hotel S21 3YB**
   Tel: 01246 432315
   A6135, right cross roads, left at spinkhill

6. **The Prince Of Wales (Guest House) S21 3UA**
   Tel: 01246 432108
   A6135, at crossroads

7. **Morrisons Superstore & Petrol S43 3UL**
   Tel: 01246 475649
   A616, A619, in Staveley

M1 Jn 31

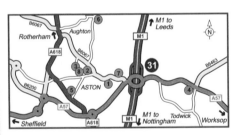

1. **Aston Hall Hotel S26 2EE**
   Tel: 0114 287 2309
   A57, immediate right B6067

2. **Aston Service Station S26 2EA**
   Tel: 0114 287 4167
   A57, immediate right B6067

3. **Rosegarth Supermarket S26 2DB**
   Tel: 0114 287 4407
   A57, immediate right B6067, left Rosegarth Av

4. **The Red Lion Inn S26 1DJ**
   Tel: 01909 771654
   A57 Worksop, 1 mile on right

5. **The Roland Arms S26 2BR**
   Tel: 0114 287 6199
   A57 Sheffield, 2nd right to Aston

6. **The Royal Oak S26 3YG**
   Tel: 0114 287 2464
   A57, immediate right B6067, right to Ulley

7. **The Yellow Lion S26 2EB**
   Tel: 0114 287 2283
   A57, immediate right B6067

8. **Co-op Supermarket S26 4WB**
   A57, immediate right B6067, left Worksop Av

M1 Jn 33

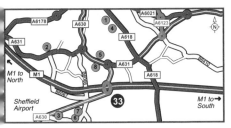

3. Burger King S60 5TR
Tel: 01709 829909
A630 South, exit lt Catcliffe, lt at r'bout, on rt

4. Oakwood Swimming Pool S60 2UE
Tel: 01709 372740
A631 East, left A618

5. Rotherham Courtyard Marriot Hotel S60 4NA
Tel: 01709 830630
North of junction on A631

6. The Plough S60 5SR
Tel: 01709 360413
A630 South, 1st exit Catcliffe, lt at T-junction

7. The Station Hotel S60 5PN
Tel: 0114 269 2631
Follow signs for Sheffield Airport, then Catcliffe + Treeton

1. BRENTWOOD HOTEL, BAR & CARVERY
Tel: 01709 382772 **S60 2TY**
26 beds e/s, conf. fclty,
150 seat rest.
A631 East, left A618

8. **halfords** **HALFORDS
S60 2XL**
Tel: 01709 820250
A631 West, on left

2. Brinsworth Service Station S60 5NU
Tel: 01709 376964
A631 West

M1 Jn 34

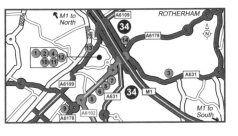

5. Premier Lodge Hotel & Restaurant S9 2YL
Tel: 0870 9906440
A6178 Meadowhall, 0.25 miles on left

6. Jet Tinsley Filling Station S9 2FY
Tel: 01142 562343
A6178 Meadowhall, on left

7. TGI Fridays Restaurant S9 2YL
Tel: 0114 2443386
A6178 Meadowhall, 0.25 miles on left

8. Pizza Hut Restaurant S9 2YZ
Tel: 0114 2562211
A6178 Sheffield, 0.5 miles on left

9. The Travel Inn S9 2LU
Tel: 0870 2383316
A6178 Sheffield, after 3rd r'bt, opp S'field Arena

1. *Meadowhall* Leisure Shopping **MEADOWHALL SHOPPING
CENTRE S9 1EP**
Tel: 0845 6006800
Award-winning shop.cntr. 270+ top stores
Signposted Meadowhall

**2. THE SOURCE AT MEADOWHALL CONFERENCE/
TRAINING CENTRE S9 1EA**
Tel: 0114 2635600
Conf/train. ctr - various rooms for hire
Signposted Meadowhall

10. **MCDONALD'S RESTAURANT
S9 1EP**
Tel: 0114 2568039
Signposted Meadowhall

11. Burger King S9 1EJ
Tel: 0114 256 8487
Signposted Meadowhall

3. THE FAIRWAYS HOTEL & RESTAURANT
Tel: 01709 838111 **S60 5NU**
8 e/s bedrooms, trad. English carvery
A631 East, 1 mile on left before golf club

12. KFC Restaurant S9 1EP
Tel: 0114 256 8197
Signposted Meadowhall

13. Rac Auto Windscreens S9 1DH
Tel: 0114 243 3633
Under Viaduct, left at r'bout, right, left

4. Sainsbury's Superstore & Petrol Station S9 1EQ
Tel: 0114 2568684
Follow signs for Hypermarket, Meadowhall Centre

14. Don Valley Diner Café and Take Away S9 1RD
Tel: 07708 864728
See sign at North-bound exit, 4th exit

M1 Jn 35

1. **ASDA CHAPELTOWN S35 2UW**
Tel: 0114 2461146
A629 Chapeltown, rt at r'bout, lt to Arundel Rd

2. The Effingham Arms Hotel S61 2AB
Tel: 01709 382094
A629 Rotherham, 1.5 miles on left

3. Scholes Service Station S61 2TA
Tel: 0114 246 7124
A629 Rotherham, 1 mile on left

4. Tesco Express Store & Petrol Forecourt S35 1SA
Tel: 0114 260 7200
A629 Chapeltown, 1.5 miles on left

5. The Travellers Inn Pub & Restaurant S61 2SE
Tel: 0114 246 7870
A629 Chapeltown, on right

6. The Regency Hotel S35 9XB
Tel: 0114 246 7703
A629 Chapeltown, 1st lt, lt at crossrds, on rt

7. Coach & Horses Hotel S35 2XE
Tel: 0114 246 7595
A629 Chapeltown, at r'bout

8. KFC Restaurant S35 1SF
Tel: 0114 257 7055
A629 Chapeltown

9. Morrisons Supermarket S35 9WJ
Tel: 0114 245 6545
A629 Chapeltown, 1st left, at crossroads

10. Spar S35 1SF
Tel: 0114 257 1091
A629 Chapeltown

11. Steadfast Tyre Co S35 1TE
Tel: 0114 245 5200
A629 Chapeltown

12. Pizza Hut S35 2UQ
A629 Chapeltown

M1 Jn 36

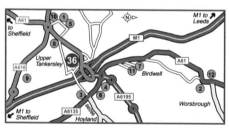

1. **SHELL WENTWORTH PARK SERVICE STATION**
Tel: 01226 350479 **S75 3DL**
Bunkering fuel key/Securicore/UK Shell
A61 Sheffield, 0.5 miles on right

2. The Button Mill Inn S70 5LJ
Tel: 01226 742277
A61 East North, for 1.5 miles, opposite Country Park

3. Challenger Tyres & Exhausts Co S74 0DP
Tel: 01226 360000
A6135 South, 0.5 miles on right

4. Cross Keys Filling Station/Jet S74 0PY
Tel: 01226 743331
A6135 South, 200 yards on left

5. **MCDONALD'S RESTAURANT S75 3DL**
Tel: 01226 740025
A61 Sheffield, 0.5 miles, on right (SB) on left (NB)

6. Cross Keys Pub Restaurant S74 0PY
Tel: 01226 742277
A6135 South, 200 yards on left

7. Hill Top Service Station S70 5XB
Tel: 01226 284412
A61 North, in Birdwell

8. Tankersley Manor Hotel S75 3DQ
Tel: 01226 744700
A61 towards Sheffield, 0.5 miles on left

9. Tankersley Park Golf Club S35 4LG
Tel: 0114 246 8247
A61 Sheffield, left A616

10. Travel Inn & Brewsters S75 3DL
Tel: 01226 350035
A61 Sheffield for 1 mile, on right at r'bout

11. Co-op Supermarket S70 5SW
A61 North, in Birdwell

12. Worsbrough Country Park S70 5LJ
Tel: 01226 774527
A61 North, on left

M1 Jn 37

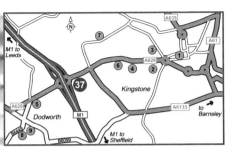

1. KFC Restaurant S70 2QX
A628 Barnsley, 3rd exit at r'bout, on right

2. **Kwik-Fit** **KWIK-FIT S70 6AB**
Tel: 01226 247623
A628 Barnsley, last exit at r'bout, on right 🔧

3. EMP Auto Electrical Centre S70 2BB
Tel: 01226 286163
A628 Barnsley, left at r'bout, left again

4. Armstrongs Restaurant S70 6HL
Tel: 01226 240113
A628 Barnsley, 1 mile on right

5. Brooklands Hotel & Conference Centre S75 3JT
Tel: 01226 299571
A628 West, 400 metres on left

6. Shell Barnsley S70 6PD
Tel: 01226 737100
A628 Barnsley

7. Intake 1 Filling Station S75 2DZ
Tel: 01226 286424
A628 Barnsley, 2nd left, 2nd right ♿

8. Travellers Inn S75 3RR
Tel: 01226 284173
A628 West, left onto B6449, on left

9. Dilraj Restaurant S75 3RF
A628 West, left B6449

M1 Jn 38

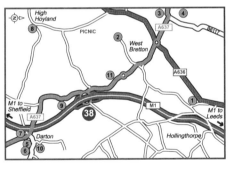

1. **BLACKER HALL FARM SPECIALITY FOOD SHOP**
Tel: 01924 267202 **WF4 3DN**
Home prod. fresh meat, baking & delicat.
A637 Huddersfield, right at r'bout, signposted ☕ ✗

2. Yorkshire Sculpture Park & Gardens WF4 4LG
Tel: 01924 832631
A637 Huddersfield, left at r'bout as signposted ♿

3. Midgley Lodge Motel WF4 4JJ
Tel: 01924 830069
A637 Huddersfield, on left ♿

4. The Black Bull Restaurant WF4 4JJ
Tel: 01924 830260
A637 North, 2 miles on right ♿

5. Cd's Cafe S75 5HQ
Tel: 01226 383939
A637 South, left into Darton, on right

6. Darton Balti Restaurant S75 5HQ
Tel: 01226 388484
A637 South, left Darton, on right

7. Rose & Crown Hotel S75 5NQ
Tel: 01226 382352
A637 Barnsley, 1.5 miles on right ♿

8. The Cherry Tree Inn S75 4BE
Tel: 01226 382541
A637 N, imm. lt, lt T-junction, in High Hoyland

9. The Old Post Office (Public House) S75 4DE
Tel: 01226 387619
A637 Barnsley, immediate left ♿

10. The Royal Spice Indian Restaurant S75 5HT
Tel: 01226 391801
A637 South, left Darton, on left

11. Bretton Country Park WF4 4LG
Tel: 01924 830550
A637 North, on left

M1 Jn 39

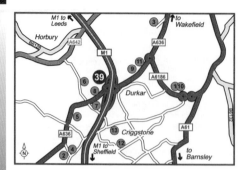

1. **ASDA** **ASDA WAKEFIELD WF2 7EQ**
Tel: 01924 259613
A636 Wakefield, last exit at r'bout, on left

2. BLACKER HALL FARM SPECIALITY FOOD SHOP
Tel: 01924 267202   WF4 3DN
Home prod. fresh meat, baking & delicat.
A636 South, 2nd lt after viaduct, signposted

3. CAMPANILE HOTEL & RESTAURANT WF2 7AL
Tel: 01924 201054
Hotel with convivial & family atmosphere
A636 W'field, 2 miles on lt, past river, turn lt

4. The Station Public House WF4 3ER
Tel: 01924 259544
A636 South, after 1 mile lt, 1st lt, on rt

5. The British Oak Inn WF4 3DL
Tel: 01924 275286
A636 South, first pub on left

6. The Navigation Public House WF4 3DS
Tel: 01924 274361
A636 South, 1st right, 1st right after shops

7. Kingfishers Fish Restaurant WF4 3DA
Tel: 01924 274994
A636 South, 0.5 miles on left

8. Cedar Court Hotel WF4 3QZ
Tel: 01924 276310
A636 Denby Dale Rd

9. Express by Holiday Inn WF4 3BB
Tel: 01924 257555
A636 Wakefield, on left

10. Pugney's Country Park WF2 7EQ
Tel: 01924 386782
A636 Wakefield, follow signs

11. Grange Service Station WF4 3BB
Tel: 01924 371209
On A636 Wakefield

12. Painthorpe House Golf & Country Club WF4 3HE
Tel: 01924 255083
A636 South, lt Crigglestone, lt Painthorpe Lane

13. Toptreads Tyres WF4 3HT
Tel: 01924 257341
A636 South, left Crigglestone, left

M1 Jn 40

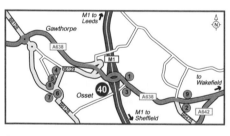

1. Days Hotel WF5 9TJ
Tel: 01924 274200
A638 Wakefield, left at lights, on right

2. **MCDONALD'S RESTAURANT WF2 9BY**
Tel: 01924 361131
A638 Wakefield, 1.5 miles on right

3. Holiday Inn WF5 9BE
Tel: 0870 400 9082
A638 Wakefield, on right

4. Mews Hotel WF5 9HN
Tel: 01924 273982
A638 West, 1st slip, left Dale St

5. Ristorante Sardegna WF5 9DB
Tel: 01924 262141
A638 West, 1st slip, left Dale St

6. Somerfield Supermarket WF5 9BT
Tel: 01924 275363
A638 West, 1st slip, left to Dale St

7. Star Of India WF5 8ER
Tel: 01924 263382
A638 West, 1st slip, left Dale St

8. Co-op Supermarket WF5 9DB
A638 West, 1st slip, left Dale St

9. Morrisons Superstore WF2 9BY
Tel: 01924 201655
A638 Wakefield

M1 Jn 41

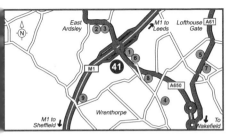

1. Carr Gate Garden Centre WF2 0SY
   Tel: 01924 823002
   A650 Wakefield, on left

2. BP Manor Service Station WF3 2HE
   Tel: 01924 872543
   A650 North ♿

3. The Bay Horse WF3 2HQ
   Tel: 01924 822262
   A650 North, on left

4. Gordon's Tyres WF1 2BE
   Tel: 01924 376551
   A650 Wakefield, bear left Bradford Rd, on left

5. Kirklands Hotel WF1 2LU
   Tel: 01924 826666
   A650 South, left A61

6. Malt Shovel Inn WF2 0QW
   Tel: 01924 875520
   A650 Wakefield, left, right, on left

7. The Empire Restaurant WF1 2DX
   Tel: 01924 870002
   A650 South, left A61

8. The Poplars Guest House WF2 0QL
   Tel: 01924 375682
   A650 South, 1st left Bradford Rd

9. The Star Inn Pub Restaurant WF2 0RZ
   Tel: 01924 374431
   A650 South, 1st left, dbl back, left Brandy Carr Rd

M1 Jn 44

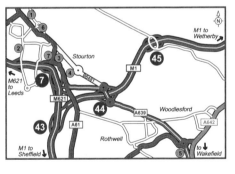

1. **MCDONALD'S RESTAURANT**
   LS10 1QR
   Tel: 01132 776262
   A61 Hunslet, 2 miles on right

2. Morrisons Superstore LS10 2AP
   Tel: 01132 704711
   A61 North, left Church St

3. **THE QUEENS HOTEL B & B LS10 1SF**
   Tel: 01132 704519
   Friendly public house, food till 7pm
   A61 North, on right

4. M & S Tyres LS10 1SW
   Tel: 01132 714318
   B6481, on left

5. Oulton Hall De Vere Hotel LS26 8HN
   Tel: 01132 821000
   A639 South, after 1 mile, rt at r'bout, on lt

6.  **KWIK-FIT**
   LS10 1RH
   Tel: 01132 700117
   A61 North, 2 miles on right

7. Fuelforce Petrol LS10 1DP
   Tel: 0113 270 9842
   On A61 North

M1 Jn 45

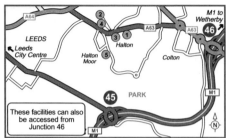

These facilities can also be accessed from Junction 46

1. Co-Op LS15 0LF
   Tel: 0113 232 6123
   West from junction, right, right A63

2. Maxwell's Restaurant LS15 7JR
   Tel: 0113 260 5098
   West from junction, right, right A63

3. Troy Autopoint Tyres LS15 0QL
   Tel: 0113 260 8464
   West from junction, right, right A63

4. Pizza Hut LS15 0QL
   Tel: 0113 260 0300
   West from junction, right, right A63

5. Temple Newsam Golf Club LS15 0LN
   Tel: 0113 264 5624
   West from junction, right, right A63, right fork in Halton

M1 Jn 46

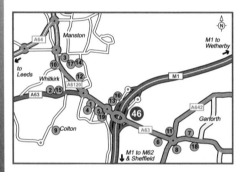

1. **MCDONALD'S RESTAURANT LS15 9JA**
   Tel: 0113 2649514
   A63 Cross Gates, on left after r'bout

2. Travel Inn Leeds East LS15 7AY
   Tel: 08701 977151
   A6120 Cross Gates, 2nd exit, 2nd r'bout

3. Crossgate Shopping Centre LS15 8ET
   Tel: 0113 2649589
   A6120 Cross Gates, 1.5 miles on right

4. Travelodge Leeds East LS15 9JA
   Tel: 0870 1911734
   A63 Cross Gates, on left after r'bout

5. Pizza Hut LS15 9JB
   Tel: 0113 2649990
   A63 Cross Gates, on left after r'bout

6. Strikes Garden Centre LS15 4LQ
   Tel: 0113 2862981
   A63 Garforth

7. Gaping Goose Inn LS25 1LR
   Tel: 0113 286 2127
   A63 Selby, on left after r'bout

8. Hilton LS25 1LH
   Tel: 0113 286 6556
   A63 Garforth, 1 mile on right

9. Home Farm (visitor attraction) LS15 0AD
   Tel: 0113 264 5535
   A63 West, left Colton

10. KFC Restaurant LS15 7JY
    Tel: 0113 264 9433
    A6120 Cross Gates, 1.5 miles on left

11. Old George Restaurant LS25 1NB
    Tel: 0113 286 2100
    A63 East

12. Sorrento Italian Restaurant LS15 8LJ
    Tel: 0113 225 2552
    A6120 West

13. Star Service Stations LS15 8QN
    Tel: 0113 284 0100
    West of junction

14. Tesco Supermarket LS15 8EU
    Tel: 0845 677 9178
    A6120 West

15. The Brown Cow LS15 7AY
    Tel: 0113 264 6112
    A6120 Cross Gates, 2nd exit of 2nd r'bout

16. Thorpe Park Hotel LS15 8ZB
    Tel: 0113 264 1000
    A63 Leeds East, right at r'bout

17. Wimpy LS15 8ET
    Tel: 0113 264 0180
    A6120 West

18. Garforth West Service Station LS25 1LP
    Tel: 0113 286 2979
    A63 East

19. Sainsburys Supermarket LS15 9JB
    Tel: 0113 232 8151
    A63 Cross Gates, on left after r'bout

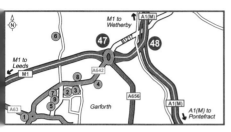

4. Aagrah Restaurant LS25 2HF
   Tel: 0113 287 6606
   A642 South

5. Garforth Balti House LS25 1DS
   Tel: 0113 287 4250
   A642 South, left Main St

6. Garforth Golf Club LS25 2DS
   Tel: 0113 286 3308
   A642 South, turn right Barwick Rd

7. Myrtle House (Guest House) LS25 1AN
   Tel: 0113 286 6445
   A642 South

8. Safeway Supermarket LS25 2DX
   Tel: 0113 287 3145
   A642 Garforth, on right

9. Tesco Supermarket LS25 1AF
   Tel: 0845 677 9290
   A642, left Main Street

1. Hilton National Leeds Garforth LS25 1LH
   Tel: 0113 2866556
   A642 Garforth for 2 miles, on right after r'bout

2. The Gascoignes LS25 1PX
   Tel: 0113 2862451
   A642 Garforth, on left

3. The Miners Arms LS25 1PX
   Tel: 0113 286 2105
   A642 Garforth, on left

M3 Summary

	1	**Sunbury A308** .... *Page 27*
		6 miles
No Accessible Facilities	**2**	**M25**
		7 miles
	3	**Woking, Bracknell A322** ...... *Page 27*
		5 miles
	4	**Camberley, A331** .... *Page 28*
		2 miles
	4a	**Farnborough A327** .... *Page 28*
		3 miles
	●	**Fleet Services**
		4 miles
	5	**Hook, A287 Farnham** .... *Page 29*
		5 miles
	6	**Basingstoke A339** .... *Page 29*
		5 miles
	7	**Basingstoke A30** .... *Page 30*
		2 miles
No Accessible Facilities	**8**	**Andover A303**
		6 miles
	●	**Winchester Services**
		4 miles
	9	**Winchester A34** .... *Page 30*
		2 miles
No Accessible Facilities	**10**	**Winchester B3330**
		2 miles
	11	**Winchester A3090** .... *Page 31*
		4 miles
	12	**Eastleigh A335** .... *Page 31*
		2 miles
	13	**Eastleigh A335** .... *Page 32*
		1 mile
No Accessible Facilities	**14**	**Southampton A33, M27**

Total Dist. **= 60 miles**

M3 Jn 1

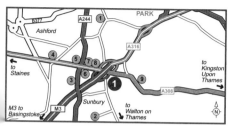

1. Curry Nights Restaurant TW13 4PJ
   Tel: 020 87513300
   Take Vicarage Rd exit at r'bout

2. Hazelwood Golf Centre TW16 6QU
   Tel: 01932 770932
   Take Green St exit at r'bout

3. Malik's Indian Restaurant TW16 7HB
   Tel: 01932 781818
   A308 West, left A244

4. Pizza Hut TW15 1RP
   Tel: 01784 240506
   A308 West

5. Sunbury Tyre Care Specialists TW16 7BH
   Tel: 01932 785242
   A308 West

6. Tesco Supermarket TW16 7BB
   Tel: 0845 677 9647
   A308 West, immediately on left

7. Total Petrol Station TW16 7BQ
   Tel: 01932 781715
   A308 West

8. Yum Yum Tree (Chinese Restaurant) TW16 7AB
   Tel: 01932 783585
   A308 West

9. BP Express TW16 5AW
   Tel: 01932 750099
   A308 East

M3 Jn 3

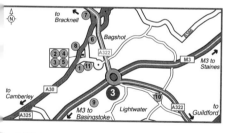

1. Bel Vedere Restaurant GU19 5AG
   Tel: 01276 475583
   A322 N, lt at lights, rt at r'bout, follow High St

2. Hardy's Mexican Restaurant GU19 5AX
   Tel: 01276 477477
   A322 North, left A30, left Bridge Rd

3. Jacks Of Bagshot Restaurant GU19 5HL
   Tel: 01276 473193
   A322 North, left A30

4. Princess Cottage Indian Restaurant GU19 5AH
   Tel: 01276 474524
   A322 North, left A30, left Bridge Rd

5. Safeway Petrol Station GU19 5HL
   Tel: 01276 476469
   A322 North, left A30

6. The Barn At Pantiles Restaurant GU19 5HN
   Tel: 01276 476673
   A322 North, left A30, on left

7. The Cricketers Restaurant GU19 5HR
   Tel: 0870 197 7021
   A322 North, on A30

8. The Mogul Indian Restaurant GU19 5HJ
   Tel: 01276 475114
   A322 North, left A30

9. Lightwater Country Park GU18 5RG
   Tel: 01276 479582
   A322 South, right Guildford Rd, right The Avenue

10. BP Petrol Station GU18 5SD
    Tel: 01276 473114
    A322 South, right Guildford Rd

11. Somerfield Supermarket GU19 5AY
    Tel: 01276 472603
    A322 North, left at lights, right at r'bout

M3 Jn 4

1. Ancient Raj Indian Restaurant GU16 7HY
   Tel: 01276 63283
   A331 South, left at r'bout, Frimley High St

2. BP Petrol Station GU14 8BD
   Tel: 01252 524457
   A331 South, right A325

3. Frimley Tandoori Restaurant GU16 7HJ
   Tel: 01276 685537
   A331 South, left A325, right at r'bout

4. **halfords** **HALFORDS**
   GU14 8BL
   Tel: 01252 372903
   A331 South, right A335, left slip road

5. Pizza Hut GU15 2QN
   Tel: 01276 675676
   A331 South, left A325, left B3411

6. Sainsburys Supermarket GU15 3YN
   Tel: 01276 676829
   A331 South, left A325, left B3411, left

7. The Peking Inn GU15 2QN
   Tel: 01276 26674
   A331 South, left A325, left B3411

8. Villa Bianca Italian Restaurant GU16 7JF
   Tel: 01276 62879
   A331 South, left A325, right at r'bout

9. Waitrose Supermarket GU16 7JD
   Tel: 01276 27477
   A331 South, left A325, right at r'bout

10. **MCDONALD'S RESTAURANT**
    GU14 8BL
    Tel: 01252 371993A331
    A331 South, A325 South

11. Olympic Greek Restaurant GU15 2QN
    Tel: 01276 684919
    A331 South, left A325, left B3411

M3 Jn 4a

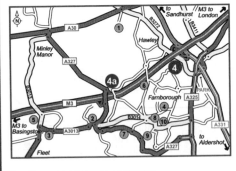

1. Abbacus Bed & Breakfast GU17 9JJ
   Tel: 01276 38339
   A327 N, rt on A30, sharp rt at r'bout, Woodside Rd

2. Harvester GU51 2SH
   Tel: 01252 816655
   A327 South, at r'bout

3. Heron On The Lakes Restaurant GU51 2RY
   Tel: 01252 812522
   A327 South, A3013, on left

4. Mobile Tyre Service GU14 8PN
   Tel: 01252 376432
   A327 S, B3014, 3rd exit at r'bout, lt Clouston Rd

5. North Hants Golf Club GU51 1RF
   Tel: 01252 616443
   A327 South, A3013, right at end, on left

6. Popadoms Anglo-Indian Brasserie GU14 9LY
   Tel: 01252 376869
   A327 S, B3014, 2nd exit at r'bout, lt to Medway Dv

7. Safeway Supermarket GU14 0NA
   Tel: 01252 377263
   Follow A327 South, on right

8. The Potters Arms GU14 0HJ
   Tel: 01252 372816
   A327 South, B3014, on left

9. Travel Inn & Brewers Fayre GU14 0JP
   Follow A327 South, on left

10. Total Petrol Station GU14 0HS
    Tel: 01252 744940
    A327 South, B3014, on left

M3 Jn 5

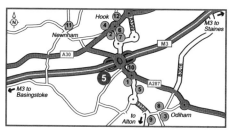

1. Blubeckers Eating House RG29 1ET
   Tel: 01256 702953
   A287 South, right at r'bout

2. Hook Tandoori Restaurant RG27 9HE
   Tel: 01256 764979
   Follow signs for Hook, left Station Rd

3. Kings Chinese Restaurant RG29 1LF
   Tel: 01256 703811
   A287 South, right at r'bout, left B3349, left High St

4. Oaklea Guest House RG27 9LA
   Tel: 01256 762673
   A287 North, right A30

5. Q8 Petrol Station RG29 1EU
   Tel: 01256 701620
   A287 South, right at r'bout

6. Raven Hotel RG27 9HS
   Tel: 01256 762541
   B3349 North, left at r'bout - Station Rd

7. Tesco Supermarket RG27 9JE
   Tel: 0845 677 9352
   B3349 North, left at r'bout - Station Rd

8. The George Hotel RG29 1LP
   Tel: 01256 702081
   A287 South, right at 2nd r'bout

9. The Grape Vine Restaurant RG29 1LA
   Tel: 01256 701122
   A287 South, right at 2nd r'bout

10. The Lord Derby Inn RG29 1HD
    Tel: 01256 702283
    A287 Odiham, 1st left at island.

11. The Old House At Home RG27 9AH
    Tel: 01256 762222
    A287 North, signs for Newham

12. White Hart Hotel RG27 9DZ
    Tel: 01256 762462
    A287 North, right A30

M3 Jn 6

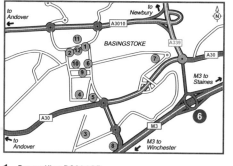

1. Burger King RG21 7BE
   Tel: 01256 321256
   A339, left A3010, left at r'bout

2. Café Rouge French Restaurant RG21 7DZ
   Tel: 01256 334556
   A30 West, right at r'bout, left London St

3. Copper Beeches Hotel RG21 3EY
   Tel: 01256 328528
   A30 Alton, left r'bout, right 2 r'bouts

4. Fernbank Hotel RG21 3DR
   Tel: 01256 321191
   A30 West, right at r'bout, 1st left

5. Fordyce Guest House RG21 3AF
   Tel: 01256 468461
   A30 West, right at r'bout

6. Galletto Italian Eatery RG21 7PG
   Tel: 01256 352622
   A30 West, right at r'bout, left London St

7. Hilton (Basingstoke) RG21 3PR
   Tel: 01256 460460
   A30 West, on right

8. Holiday Inn RG21 3EE
   Tel: 0870 400 9004
   A30 West, left at r'bout

9. KWIK-FIT
   RG21 3DZ
   Tel: 01256 329966
   A30 West, right at r'bout, left Southern Rd

10. MCDONALD'S RESTAURANT
    RG21 7QA
    Tel: 01256 811973
    A30 West, right at r'bout onto London Rd

11. Pizza Hut RG21 7BE
    Tel: 01256 476666
    A339, left A3010, left at r'bout

12. The Bengal Brasserie RG21 7DY
    Tel: 01256 332847
    A30 West, right at r'bout, left London St

M3 Jn 7

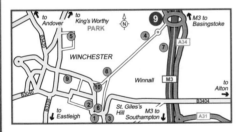

1. Basingstoke Golf Club RG23 7LL
   Tel: 01256 351332
   A30 North, on right

2. Beeches Guest House RG22 5LL
   Tel: 01256 325150
   A30 North, lt at 2nd r'bout, 1st rt, 3rd lt

3. Sainsburys Supermarket RG22 4TW
   Tel: 01256 468405
   A30 North, on right

4. The Fox RG25 2BE   ♿
   Tel: 01256 397288
   A30 South, 2nd right to North Waltham, on left

5. The Queen Inn RG25 2AD
   Tel: 01256 397367
   Dummer exit of r'bout, on right

6. The Spice Indian Restaurant RG22 5HN
   Tel: 01256 356480
   A30 North, left at 3rd r'bout, on right

7. The Wheatsheaf Hotel RG25 2BB
   Tel: 01256 398282
   A30 South

8. Dummer Golf Club RG25 2AF
   At junction

M3 Jn 9

1. Bishop On The Bridge (Public House) SO23 9JX
   Tel: 01962 855111
   Easton Lane exit, left Water Lane, right High St

2. Charles House (Chinese Restaurant) SO23 8EB
   Tel: 01962 854919
   Easton Lane exit, left Union Street, on right

3. Chesil Rectory Restaurant SO23 0HU
   Tel: 01962 851555
   Easton Lane exit, left Water Lane, Chesil St

4. **halfords**   **HALFORDS SO23 7RX**
   Tel: 01962 849411
   Easton Lane exit, 2nd right, 1st left

5. King Alfred SO23 7DJ
   Tel: 01962 854370
   Easton Lane exit, right Hyde St, right King Alfred Pl,left Saxon Rd

6. Pizza Express Restaurant SO23 9BH
   Tel: 01962 841845
   Easton Lane exit, left Water Lane, right High St

7. Tesco Supermarket SO23 7RS
   Tel: 0845 677 9723
   Easton Lane exit, on left

8. The First In Last Out (Public House) SO23 0ET
   Tel: 01962 865963
   Easton Lane exit, on right

9. The Foresters Arms SO23 8DA
   Tel: 01962 861539
   Easton Lane exit, on left

10. Willow Tree SO23 8QX
    Tel: 01962 877255
    Easton Lane exit, left Durngate Terrace

M3 Jn 11

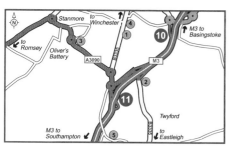

1. The Bell Inn SO23 9RJ
Tel: 01962 865284
B3335 North

2. Hockley Golf Club SO21 1PL
Tel: 01962 713165
B3335 Twyford

3. Sainsburys Supermarket SO22 4QB
Tel: 01962 867896
A3090, on right

4. St Cross Garage (Repairs) SO23 9SF
Tel: 01962 861481
B3335 North

5. The Bridge (Pub Restaurant) SO21 2BP
Tel: 01962 713171
A3090, sharp left at r'bout, in Shawford

M3 Jn 12

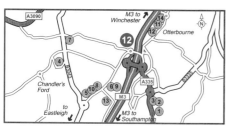

1. BP Service Station SO50 4HP
Tel: 023 80652504
A335 South

2. Travelodge SO50 4LF
Tel: 023 80616813
A335 South

3. Ham Farm Harvester SO50 4LF
Tel: 023 80619181
A335 South

4. Hiltonbury Farmhouse SO53 1SZ
Tel: 023 80269974
Take Hocombe Rd, lt Hursley Rd, rt Baddesley Rd

5. Kings Court Restaurant SO53 2GG
Tel: 023 80252232
At exit r'bout take Winchester Rd South

6. **Kwik-Fit** KWIK-FIT SO53 2DS
Tel: 023 80262045
At exit r'bout take Winchester Rd South

7. Pine Hurst Guest House SO53 5PJ
Tel: 023 80270303
Exit West on Hocombe Rd, left Hursley Rd

8. Safeway Supermarket SO53 2GH
Tel: 023 80266561
At exit r'bout take Winchester Rd South

9. Shell Service Station SO53 2DS
Tel: 023 80259990
Winchester Rd to Chandler's Ford, on left

10. Sunrise Balti & Tandoori SO53 2GG
Tel: 023 80268383
At exit r'bout take Winchester Rd South

11. The Old Forge (Pub Restaurant) SO21 2EE
Tel: 01962 717191
At exit r'bout take Winchester Rd N, Otterbourne

12. The White Horse Inn SO21 2EQ
Tel: 01962 712830
At exit r'bout take Winchester Rd N, Otterbourne

13. Waitrose Supermarket SO53 2LG
Tel: 023 80260230
At exit r'bout take Winchester Rd South

14. Williams Garage (Petrol) SO21 2EE
Tel: 01962 713150
At exit r'bout take Winchester Rd N, Otterbourne

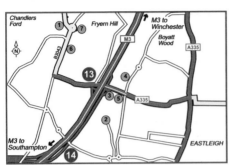

1. Fanellis Famous Pizza SO53 3DB
Tel: 023 80274727
A335 West, B3043, on left

2. Fleming Park Golf Course SO50 9LH
Tel: 023 80612797
A335 East, turn right, on right

3. Travel Inn & Brewers Fayre SO50 9YX
Tel: 0870 197 7090
A335 East, on right

4. halfords **HALFORDS**
SO50 9NA
Tel: 023 80629655
A335 East, turn left, on left

5. Holiday Inn Eastleigh SO50 9PG
Tel: 0870 400 9075
A335 East, on right

6. Rapid Fit SO53 3DH
Tel: 023 80271000
A335 West, B3043, on right

7. Thai Cottage Restaurant SO53 2GA
Tel: 023 80266830
A335 West, B3043, on right

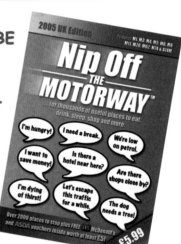

M4 Summary

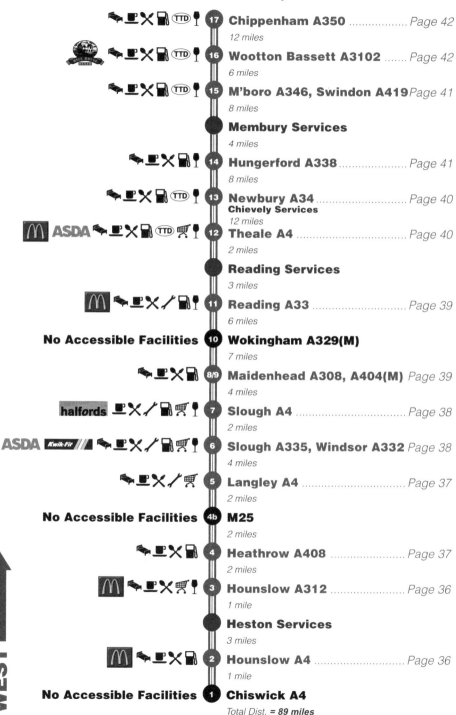

🛏️🚹✕🖪ⓉⓉⒹ🍴 **17** **Chippenham A350** .... *Page 42*
12 miles

🛏️🚹✕🖪ⓉⓉⒹ🍴 **16** **Wootton Bassett A3102** .... *Page 42*
6 miles

🛏️🚹✕🖪ⓉⓉⒹ🍴 **15** **M'boro A346, Swindon A419** *Page 41*
8 miles

● **Membury Services**
4 miles

🛏️🚹✕🖪🍴 **14** **Hungerford A338** .... *Page 41*
8 miles

🛏️🚹✕🖪ⓉⓉⒹ🍴 **13** **Newbury A34** .... *Page 40*
Chievely Services
12 miles

Ⓜ **ASDA** 🛏️🚹✕🖪ⓉⓉⒹ🛒🍴 **12** **Theale A4** .... *Page 40*
2 miles

● **Reading Services**
3 miles

Ⓜ 🛏️🚹✕🔧🖪🍴 **11** **Reading A33** .... *Page 39*
6 miles

No Accessible Facilities **10** **Wokingham A329(M)**
7 miles

🛏️🚹✕🖪 **8/9** **Maidenhead A308, A404(M)** *Page 39*
4 miles

halfords 🚹✕🔧🖪🛒🍴 **7** **Slough A4** .... *Page 38*
2 miles

ASDA **Kwik-Fit** 🛏️🚹✕🔧🖪🛒🍴 **6** **Slough A335, Windsor A332** *Page 38*
4 miles

🛏️🚹✕🔧🛒 **5** **Langley A4** .... *Page 37*
2 miles

No Accessible Facilities **4b** **M25**
2 miles

🛏️🚹✕🖪 **4** **Heathrow A408** .... *Page 37*
2 miles

Ⓜ 🛏️🚹✕🛒🍴 **3** **Hounslow A312** .... *Page 36*
1 mile

● **Heston Services**
3 miles

Ⓜ 🛏️🚹✕🖪 **2** **Hounslow A4** .... *Page 36*
1 mile

No Accessible Facilities **1** **Chiswick A4**
Total Dist. **= 89 miles**

WEST

Facilities	Jct	Location	Page
	35	**Bridgend, Pen-coed A473**	... *Page 48*
		6 miles	
	34	**Llantrisant, Rhonda A4119**	*Page 47*
		2 miles	
	33	**Cardiff West Services**	
		3 miles	
ASDA	**32**	**Cardiff A470**	*Page 47*
		5 miles	
ASDA	**30**	**Cardiff A4232**	*Page 46*
		Cardiff Gate Services	
		3 miles	
No Accessible Facilities	**29**	**Cardiff A48M**	
		2 miles	
ASDA	**28**	**Rogerstone A467**	*Page 46*
		1 mile	
	27	**Risca B4591**	*Page 45*
		2 miles	
Kwik-Fit	**26**	**Cwmbran A4051**	*Page 45*
		1 mile	
No Accessible Facilities	**25a**	**Newport A4042**	
		0 miles	
No Accessible Facilities	**25**	**Caerleon B4596**	
		3 miles	
	24	**Newport A48**	*Page 44*
		4 miles	
	23a	**Magor, Caldicot B4245**	.... *Page 44*
		Magor Services	
		1 mile	
No Accessible Facilities	**23**	**M48**	
		7 miles	
No Accessible Facilities	**22**	**M49**	
		3 miles	
No Accessible Facilities	**21**	**M48**	
		2 miles	
No Accessible Facilities	**20**	**M5**	
		3 miles	
HILL HOUSE	**19**	**M32**	*Page 43*
		7 miles	
Kwik-Fit	**18**	**Bath, A46**	*Page 43*
		9 miles	
		Leigh Delamere Services	
		2 miles	
	17	**Chippenham A350**	*Page 42*
		Total Dist. = 66 miles	

No Facilities Listed **(49) Carmarthen A48, Services**
3 miles

🛏️🍵(TTD)🛒🍷 **(48) Pontarddullais, Llanelli A4183** *Page 53*
4 miles

M 🛏️🍵✕🛢️🍷 **(47) Swansea A483** .... *Page 53*
Swansea West Services
2 miles

No Accessible Facilities **(46) Swansea B4489, A48**
2 miles

M 🛏️🍵✕(TTD)🛒🌊🍷 **(45) Swansea, A4067** .... *Page 52*
2 miles

ASDA halfords 🛏️🍵✕🔧🛢️🛒🍷 **(44) Swansea A48** .... *Page 52*
2 miles

🍵✕🔧🛒 **(43) Neath A465** .... *Page 51*
2 miles

🛏️🛢️(TTD) **(42) Briton Ferry, Swansea A483** *Page 51*
3 miles

M 🛏️🍵✕🔧(TTD)🛒🌊🍷 **(41) Port Talbot A48** .... *Page 50*
1 mile

🛏️🍵✕🛢️🛒 **(40) Port Talbot A4107** .... *Page 50*
4 miles

🛏️🍵✕(TTD)🍷 **(38/39) Port Talbot A48** .... *Page 49*
3 miles

🛏️🍵✕🛢️(TTD)🌊🍷 **(37) Pyle, Porthcawl A4229** .... *Page 49*
6 miles

🛏️🍵✕(TTD)🌊🍷 **(36) Bridgend A4061, A4063** .... *Page 48*
Sarn Park Services
4 miles

🛏️🍵✕🛢️(TTD)🌊🍷 **(35) Bridgend, Pen-coed A473** .... *Page 48*

Total Dist. = 38 miles

WEST ⬆

M4 Jn 2

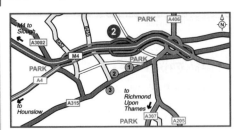

2. | MCDONALD'S RESTAURANT
TW8 0JS
Tel: 020 82328496
On A315 West off junction

3. Premier Lodge TW8 0BB
Tel: 0870 990 6304
On A315 West

1. Brentford Filling Station TW8 0DU
Tel: 020 85688244
On A315 West

M4 Jn 3

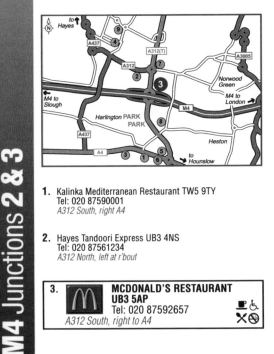

1. Kalinka Mediterranean Restaurant TW5 9TY
Tel: 020 87590001
A312 South, right A4

2. Hayes Tandoori Express UB3 4NS
Tel: 020 87561234
A312 North, left at r'bout

3. MCDONALD'S RESTAURANT
UB3 5AP
Tel: 020 87592657
A312 South, right to A4

4. New Bowl Chinese Restaurant UB3 1AX
Tel: 020 85738068
A312 N, lt at r'bout, rt Station Rd, lt Clayton Rd

5. Ramada Jarvis Hotel TW5 9QE
Tel: 020 88972121
A312 South, right A4

6. Sharma Tandoori TW5 9TY
Tel: 020 87590424
A312 South, right A4

7. Tesco Supermarket UB2 5LN
Tel: 0845 677 9338
A312 North

8. The Cottage (Guest House) TW5 9WB
Tel: 020 88971815
A312 South, left High St

9. MCDONALD'S RESTAURANT
UB3 4DD
Tel: 020 85739328
A312 North, left at r'bout, right Station Rd

M4 Jn 4

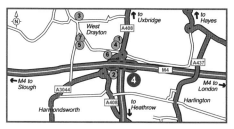

1. Crowne Plaza Hotel UB7 9NA
Tel: 0870 400 9140
2nd exit at r'bout

2. Holiday Inn UB7 0JU
Tel: 0870 400 8595
1st exit at r'bout, left at next r'bout

3. S T C Petrol Station UB7 7ND
Tel: 01895 445488
2nd exit at r'bout, right Station Rd

4. Simply Nico (French Restaurant) UB7 9NA
Tel: 01895 437564
2nd exit at r'bout, in Crowne Plaza

5. Sipson Tandoori UB7 9JJ
Tel: 01895 435515
2nd exit at r'bout, left Harmondsworth Rd

6. Novotel London Heathrow UB7 9HJ
2nd exit at r'bout, on left

7. Zee Café UB7 9DP
Tel: 01895 430520
2nd exit at r'bout, on left

M4 Jn 5

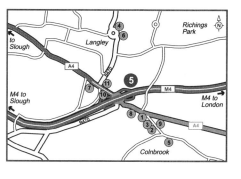

1. Airport Guest House SL3 8QF
Tel: 01753 685319
A4 South, on right

2. Aston Hotel SL3 8QH
Tel: 01753 734047
A4 South, right fork

3. Brands Hill Lodge Guest House SL3 8QF
Tel: 01753 680377
A4 South, right fork

4. Budgens Stores SL3 8HJ
Tel: 01753 546592
A4 North, B470, on right

5. Cedars Guest House SL3 0JZ
Tel: 01753 681058
A4 South, right Colnbrook

6. India Tandoori SL3 8HN
Tel: 01753 542889
A4 North, B470, on right

7. Harvester (Restaurant) SL3 7HX
Tel: 01753 543009
A4 North

8. Motorist Discount Centre SL3 8QR
Tel: 01753 540113
A4 South

9. Regent House Hotel SL3 8QG
Tel: 01753 683093
A4 South, right fork

10. Slough Windsor Marriott Hotel SL3 8PT
Tel: 0870 400 7244
A4 North

11. Toby Carvery SL3 8PS
Tel: 01753 591212
A4 North

M4 Jn 6

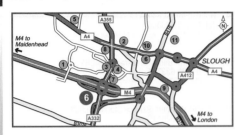

4. Courtyard By Marriott Hotel SL1 2NH
Tel: 01753 551551
A355 North, on right

5. Fuelforce Petrol Station SL1 4DX
Tel: 01753 533021
A355 North, left A4, on right

6. **Kwik-Fit** **KWIK-FIT SL1 3UA**
Tel: 01753 528414
A355 North, right A4

7. Murco Petroleum Ltd SL1 2TW
Tel: 01753 532587
A355 North, right r'bout, right High Street

8. Pizza Hut SL1 3UW
Tel: 01753 573373
A355 Slough, after r'bout left at lights

9. Upton Park Hotel SL1 2DA
Tel: 01753 528797
A355 North, rt A4, rt r'bout, lt Upton Park

10. Al Samit Hotel (Guest House) SL1 3SG
A355 North, right A4, left Landsdowne Road

11. Tesco Supermarket
Tel: 0845 677 9629
A355 North, right A4, left after r'about

1. **ASDA** **ASDA SLOUGH SL1 9LA** £
Tel: 01753 524017
A355 North, left at r'bout, left Telford Drive

2. Barn Tandoori SL1 3SR
Tel: 01753 553072
A355 North, right A4

3. Copthorne Hotel SL1 2YE
Tel: 01753 516222
A355 North, on left

M4 Jn 7

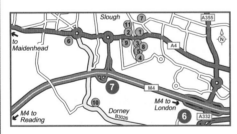

5. Prince Of India SL1 5QS
Tel: 01628 663899
A4 East, right Elmshot Lane

6. Sainsburys Supermarket SL6 0QH
Tel: 01628 661529
A4 West, at r'bout

7. Shell Petrol Station SL1 6LP
Tel: 01628 600000
A4 East, left at Burnham Lane

8. Somerfield Supermarket SL1 5QS
Tel: 01628 661044
A4 East, right at Elmshot Lane

9. The Kai-Leung Chinese Restaurant SL1 6AA
Tel: 01628 666411
A4 East, on right

10. The Palmer Arms SL4 6QW
Tel: 01628 666612
Left A4, 2nd left, left

11. Tummies Bistro SL1 6JJ
Tel: 01628 668486
A4 East, left Station Road

1. **halfords** **HALFORDS SL1 6JA**
Tel: 01628 603312
A4 East, on left

2. Hi-Q Tyre Services SL1 6BB
Tel: 01628 663237
A4 East, on left

3. KFC Restaurant SL1 5QL
Tel: 01628 603020
A4 East, on right

4. National Tyres And Autocare SL1 5QU
Tel: 01628 602222
A4 East, right Elmshot Lane

M4 Jn 8/9

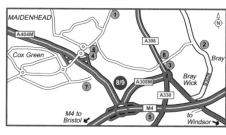

1. **Fredricks Hotel & Restaurant SL6 2PZ**
   Tel: 01628 635934
   A404M, 1st exit, head North of motorway, on right

2. **The Fat Duck (Restaurant) SL6 2AQ**
   Tel: 01628 580333
   A308M, A308 Windsor, left B3028, on right

3. **Braywick Service Station SL6 1UZ**
   Tel: 01628 623315
   A308M, A308 North, on right

4. **Holiday Inn SL6 2RA**
   Tel: 01628 506000
   A404M, 1st exit, head North of motorway at r'bout

5. **Moor Farm Bed & Breakfast SL6 2HY**
   Tel: 01628 633761
   A308M, A330 Bracknell/Ascot. on right

6. **Shoppenhangers Service Station SL6 2QJ**
   Tel: 01628 626110
   A404M, 1st exit, N of m/way, next to Holiday Inn

7. **The Farrier (Restaurant) SL6 3AA**
   Tel: 01628 777428
   A404M, 1st exit, S of m/way, lt at r'bt, lt at T-J

8. **The Stag At Bray (Indian Restaurant) SL6 1UZ**
   Tel: 01628 624100
   A308M, left A308, on right

M4 Jn 11

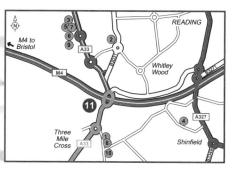

1. **Eurotec Tyres RG7 1BA**
   Tel: 0118 988 6153
   A33 South, left at r'bout

2. **Holiday Inn RG2 0SL**
   Tel: 0870 400 9067
   B3031, at r'bout

3. **KFC Restaurant RG2 0QG**
   Tel: 0118 986 0856
   A33 North

4. **L'Ortolan French Restaurant RG2 9BY**
   Tel: 0118 988 3783
   A33 South, lt at r'bout, 1st lt, rt Shinfield

5. **MCDONALD'S RESTAURANT**
   RG2 0QG
   Tel: 0118 975 2343
   A33 North

6. **Millennium Madejski Hotel RG2 0FL** &
   Tel: 0118 925 3500
   A33 North. Follow signs Madejski Stadium

7. **Pizza Hut RG2 0QG**
   Tel: 0118 987 1798
   A33 North

8. **Quantum Filling Station RG7 1BA**
   Tel: 0118 988 2334
   A33 South, left at r'bout

9. **The Jazz Cafe RG2 0FL** &
   Tel: 0118 968 1442
   Reading Football Club Stadium

10. **The Swan - Three Mile Cross RG7 1AT**
    Tel: 0118 988 3674
    A33 South, left at r'bout

M4 Jn 12

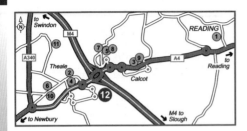

5. **MCDONALD'S RESTAURANT RG31 7SA**
Tel: 0118 941 5744
A4 East, left at r'bout

6. Old Lamb Hotel RG7 5BZ
Tel: 0118 930 2357
A4 West, on Church Street, Theale

7. Pincents Manor Hotel RG31 4UQ
Tel: 0118 932 3511
A4 East, left at r'bout

8. Sainsburys Supermarket RG31 7SA
Tel: 0118 938 2200
A4 East, left at r'bout

9. Silsila Tandoori RG31 4UT
Tel: 0118 941 7551
A4 Reading,on left at 3rd r'bout

10. The Volunteer RG7 5BX
Tel: 0118 930 2489
A4 Newbury, 1st rt, lt at r'bout, last pub on lt

11. Theale Golf Centre RG7 5EX
Tel: 0118 930 5331
Theale Village, rt at Red Lion, North Street

1. **ASDA RG30 4EL**
Tel: 0118 939 4339
A4 East, on left

2. Blue Cobra Restaurant RG7 5AN
Tel: 0118 930 4040
A4 West, off on right in Theale

3. BP Petrol Station RG31 7QN
Tel: 0118 942 7912
A4 East

4. Co-op Supermarket RG7 5AN
Tel: 0118 930 2424
A4 West

M4 Jn 13

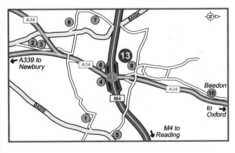

4. **MOTO HOSPITALITY LTD RG18 9XX**
Tel: 01635 248024
Vital re-fuelling for motorists
A34, Signposted

5. The Coffee House Restaurant RG18 9TG
Tel: 01635 201631
A34 North, off slip road, right

6. The Hilton RG20 8XY
Tel: 01635 247010
On A34 South

7. The Winterbourne Arms (Pub Restaurant) RG20 8BB
Tel: 01635 248200
A34 S, exit lt, over A34, rt, lt B4434, 1st rt, rt

8. Ye Olde Red Lion RG20 8XB
Tel: 01635 248379
A34 North, exit left Chievely

9. Snelsmore Common Country Park RG16 9PN
Tel: 01635 519620
A34 South, exit left, over A34, left on B4494

10. The Coach & Horses RG20 8SD
Tel: 01635 248743
A34 Beedon, 1st exit, lt, rt, 2 miles on right

1. Bunk Inn Restaurant RG18 9DS
Tel: 01635 200400
A34 S. Exit left , on right

2. Donnington Valley Hotel & Golf Club RG14 3AG
Tel: 01635 551199
A34 South, exit left, over A34, left

3. **FOX & HOUNDS INN RG14 3AP**
Tel: 01635 40540
Real food, fine ales, open all day
A34 Donnington, local Oxford Road

M4 Jn 14

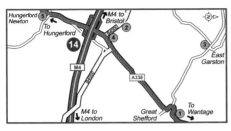

1. Brookside Filling Station RG17 7DB
Tel: 01488 648845
A338 North, on left

2. Fishers Farm Guest House RG17 7AB
Tel: 01488 648466
A338 North, left to B4000, right to Fishers Farm

3. Queens Arms Hotel RG17 7ET
Tel: 01488 648757
A338 North, left to East Garston, in village

4. The Pheasant Inn RG17 7AA
Tel: 01488 648284
A338 Wantage, left to B4000 Lambourn

5. The Tally Ho Inn RG17 0PP
Tel: 01488 682312
A338 Hungerford, 1 mile on left

M4 Jn 15

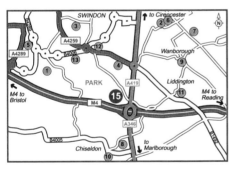

1. Broome Manor Golf Complex SN3 1RG
Tel: 01793 532403
A419 North, A4259, left B4006, turn left

2. Ducksbridge Guest House SN4 0AP
Tel: 01793 790338
A419 North, at r'bout right Wanborough, 1st left

3. King Balti Indian Restaurant SN3 2LP
Tel: 01793 423332
A419 North, left A4259, at r'bout take Shaftesbury Ave, left Whitbourne Ave

4. Kingsbridge House (Guest House) SN3 6AA
Tel: 01793 522861
A419 North, left A4259

5. Swindon Marriott Hotel SN3 1SH
Tel: 01793 512121
A419 North, left A4259, left B4006, at r'bout

6. The Cross Keys SN4 0AP   ♿
Tel: 01793 790302
A419 Swindon, right at r'bout, Wanborough, 1st left

7. The Harrow Inn Wanborough SN4 0AE
Tel: 01793 790622
A419 N, 3rd exit at r'bout, to Lower Wanborough

8. The Landmark Hotel SN4 0PW
Tel: 01793 740149
A346 South, right at Esso Garage, right Station Rd

9. The New Calley Arms SN4 0DF   ♿
Tel: 01793 790615
A419 North, 1st r'bout, take 3rd exit, on right

10. The Patriots Arms Inn SN4 0LU
Tel: 01793 740331
A346 Malborough, right Esso Garage

11. The Village Inn SN4 0HE   ♿
Tel: 01793 790314
B4192 Liddington, up hill on left

12. Holiday Inn SN3 6AQ
Tel: 0870 400 9079
A419 North, left A4259, on right

13. Shell Petrol Station SN3 1NP
Tel: 01793 489960
A419 North, left A4259, left B4006

M4 Jn 16

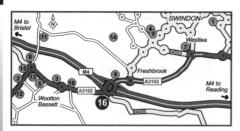

6. Hilton National Hotel SN5 8UZ
Tel: 01793 881777
A3102 East, at r'bout

7. Hotel Ibis SN5 7XG
Tel: 01793 514777
A3102 Swindon, 2nd r'bt exit to Delta Bus. Pk, lt

8. Marsh Farm Hotel SN4 8ER
Tel: 01793 848044
A3102 West, right at 2nd r'bout

9. Pizza Hut SN5 7DW
Tel: 01793 876212
A3102 Swindon, left at 1st r'bout

10. Sally Pussey's Inn SN4 8ET
Tel: 01793 852430
Take Wootton Basset, on right ᕕ

11. School House Hotel & Restaurant SN4 8EF
Tel: 01793 851198
A3102 Swindon, left at 2 r'bouts, Hook St

12. Shell Petrol Station SN4 7AS
Tel: 01793 859020
A3102 West, left at r'bout

13. Timberdale Guest House SN4 8ES
Tel: 01793 852789
A3102 West

14. Lydiard Country Park SN5 5PA ᕕ
Tel: 01793 771419
A3102 Swindon, left at 2 r'bouts, Hook St

15. The Prince Of Wales SN4 7HT
Tel: 01793 852388
A3102 Wootton Bassett, after 2 r'bouts

1. THE PATTERN STORE RESTAURANT & BAR
Tel: 01793 887710   **SN2 2BA**
Unique building, good
food & real ales   £ **HGV**
A3102 Swindon, signs outlet ♿ ▯
village, next to W car park ☕ ⊗ ✕

2. BP Petrol Station SN4 7HF
Tel: 01793 855147
A3102 West, left at r'bout

3. Churchill House Restaurant SN4 8ET
Tel: 01793 849848
A3102 West

4. De Vere Hotel SN5 7DW
Tel: 01793 878785
A3102 Swindon, left at r'bout

5. Fairview (Guest House) SN4 8EU
Tel: 01793 852283
A3102 West

M4 Jn 17

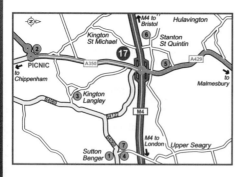

1. Bell House Hotel SN15 4RH
Tel: 01249 720401
B4122, left B4069, in Sutton Benger

2. Chippenham Golf Club SN15 5LT
Tel: 01249 655519
A350 South, on right

3. Hit Or Miss Inn SN15 5NS ᕕ
Tel: 01249 758830
A350 Chippenham, left at lights, left

4. La Flambe (French Restaurant) SN15 4RY
Tel: 01249 720247
B4122, left B4069, left in Sutton Benger

5. Murco Petroleum Ltd SN14 6BN
Tel: 01666 837161
A429, on left

6. Stanton Manor Hotel SN14 6DQ
Tel: 01666 837552
A429, first left, in Stanton St. Quintin

7. Wellesley Arms SN15 4RD
Tel: 01249 720251
B4122, left B4069, in Sutton Benger

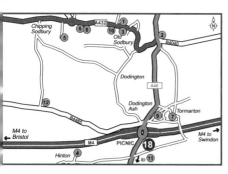

5. King Grove Farm BS37 6DY
Tel: 01454 312314
A46 North, A432, left after r'about

6.  **KWIK-FIT BS37 6LL**
Tel: 01454 321556
A46 North, A432

7. Portcullis Inn Tormarton GL9 1HZ
Tel: 01454 218263
A46 North, right Tormarton

8. The Bell Hotel BS37 6LL
Tel: 01454 313372
A46 North, A432

9. The Compass Inn GL9 1JB   ♿
Tel: 01454 218242
A46 Stroud, first right to B4465, on right

10. The Sodbury House Hotel BS37 6LU
Tel: 01454 312847
A46 Stroud, left at lights, on left

11. Tollgate Tea Shop SN14 8LF
Tel: 01225 891585
A46 Bath, on right   ♿

12. Codrington Arms BS37 6RY
Tel: 01454 313145
A46 Stroud, 1st left, on right ♿

1. Cotswold Service Station BS37 6LX
Tel: 01454 323524
A46 North, A432

2. Cross Hands Hotel BS37 6RJ
Tel: 01454 313000
A46 North

3. DOG INN & RESTAURANT BS37 6LZ ♿
Tel: 01454 312006
Traditional old world pub accommodation
A46 Stroud, left at lights, half mile left

4. Hinton Grange Hotel SN14 8HG
Tel: 0117 937 2916
A46 South, right at crossroads

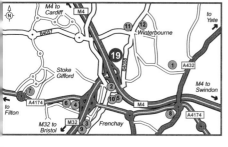

4. Hambrook Golf Range BS16 1QQ
Tel: 0117 970 1116
A4174 West, left at junction r'bout

5. Hambrook Grove Hotel BS16 1RY
Tel: 0117 956 9770
A4174 East, left B4058, rt Bristol Rd

6. Holiday Inn (Bristol Filton) BS16 1QX
Tel: 0870 400 9014
A4174 West

7. Sainsburys Supermarket BS34 8SS
Tel: 0117 923 6459
A4174 West

8. Shell Petrol Station BS36 1AH
Tel: 0117 970 9000
A4174 East, at r'bout

9. Snuff Mill Harvester Restaurant BS16 1LF
Tel: 0117 956 6560
A4174 East, right to Frenchay

10. The Coach House Guest House BS16 1RY
Tel: 0117 956 6901
A4174 East, left B4058, rt Bristol Rd

11. The Royal Raj (Pub & Indian Restaurant) BS36 1JN
Tel: 01454 773301
A4174, left B4058

12. The Wheatsheaf Inn Hotel BS36 1JG
Tel: 01454 773758
A4174 East, left B4058

1. GOLDEN HEART INN BS36 1AU
Tel: 01454 773152
Fam pub, home cooking,
big gdn, real ale
A4174 East, lt at r'bt, lt at sign in field, on rt

2. Crown Inn BS16 1RY ♿
Tel: 0117 956 6701
M32 exit 1, keep left, left at lights

3. Frenchay Park Service Station BS16 1LF
Tel: 0117 970 1977
A4174 East, right to Frenchay

M4 Jn 23a

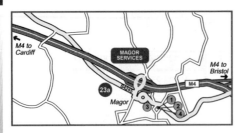

1. Angelo's Fish Bar NP26 3HU
Tel: 01633 880428
On B4245 East

2. Bella Pizzas NP26 3HY
Tel: 01633 880153
B4245 East, right Newport Rd, 2nd right

3. Old Tythe Garage (Repairs) NP26 3BZ
Tel: 01633 881091
On B4245 East

4. Mango House Restaurant NP26 3HY
Tel: 01633 882644
B4245 East, right Newport Rd, 2nd right

5. First Motorway Services (Hotel) NP26 3YL
Tel: 01633 881515
At services North of junction

M4 Jn 24

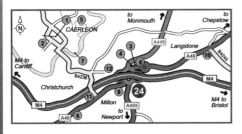

1. Bagan Tandoori Restaurant NP18 1AF
Tel: 01633 422489
A48 West, B4236 Caerleon, right Cross St

2. Caerleon Golf Course NP18 1AY
Tel: 01633 420441
A48 West, B4236 Caerleon, left off High St

3. Coldra Tyres NP18 2NX
Tel: 01633 411155
On A48 East

4. **MCDONALD'S RESTAURANT**
NP6 2LX
Tel: 01633 412087
At junction on A48 East

5. Pendragon House (Guest House) NP18 1AF
Tel: 01633 430871
A48 West, B4236 Caerleon, High St, 1st right

6. Texaco Petrol Station NP19 9EX
Tel: 01633 636900
On A48 West

7. The Bell Inn NP18 1QQ
Tel: 01633 420613
A48 West, right, right Bullmore Rd

8. The Hilton Hotel NP18 2LX
Tel: 01633 413737
North of junction on A48

9. The Holiday Inn NP18 2YG
Tel: 01633 412777
South of junction

10. The New Inn Hotel NP18 2JN
Tel: 01633 412426
On A48 East

11. Treberth Service Station NP19 9EZ
Tel: 01633 281241
On A48 West

12. The Celtic Manor Resort & Golf Club NP18 2YB
Tel: 01633 413000
A48 West, follow signs

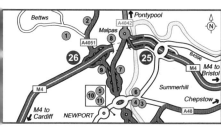

1. Bettws Leisure Centre & Pool NP20 7YB
Tel: 01633 855420
A4051 North, left for Bettws, on left

2. Borderer Harvester NP20 6EP
Tel: 01633 858667
A4051 North

3. Chez Giovanni Italian Restaurant NP19 0AH
Tel: 01633 259003
Towards Newport, left at Castle

4. DILSHAD INTERNATIONAL CUISINE NP19 0AG
Tel: 01633 256250
High class Tandoori cuisine, fully lic.
A4051 Newport, by Castle, 1st left &

5. Kings Hotel NP20 1QU
Tel: 01633 842020
A4051 South, right Newport, on High St

6. **Kwik-Fit** / **KWIK-FIT NP19 7AB**
Tel: 01633 254936
A4051 South, left by Castle, over river /

7. **McDONALD'S RESTAURANT NP20 5JG**
Tel: 01633 253433
A4051 South, left r'bout

8. Newport Lodge Hotel NP20 5QN
Tel: 01633 821818
A4051 South, left Brynglas Rd, left Bryn Bevan

9. Shell Petrol Station NP20 5PA
Tel: 01633 820000
Exit South A4051

10. Somerfield NP20 4AD
A4051 South, right Queensway, left Cambrian Rd

11. Popadoms Indian Restaurant NP20 1FQ
A4051 South, right Queensway, on High Street

M4 Jn 27

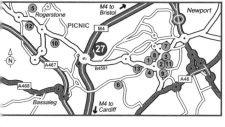

1. Cresent Guest House NP20 4HG
Tel: 01633 776677
B4591 Newport, left after lights &

2. Glenroy Hotel NP20 4HB
Tel: 01633 265541
B4591 Newport, on left

3. Kepe Lodge Guest House NP20 4HH
Tel: 01633 262351
B4591 Newport, left Caerau Road

4. Manor Hotel NP20 4FZ
Tel: 01633 264685
B4591 Newport, on right

5. Newport Golf NP10 9FX
Tel: 01633 892643
B4591 North, off on right

6. Spar NP20 3NA
Tel: 01633 266102
B4591 Newport, right Bassaleg Road

7. Spar NP20 4NZ
Tel: 01633 263147
B4591 Newport, left Caerau Road

8. The Caerleon House Hotel NP20 4HJ
Tel: 01633 264869
B4591 Newport, left Caerau Road

9. The Knoll Guest House NP20 4FZ
Tel: 01633 263557
B4591 Newport

10. The Rising Sun NP10 9AQ
Tel: 01633 895126
B4591 High Cross, on left

11. Stow Hill Service Station NP20 4GA
Tel: 01633 251500
B4591 Newport

12. Tredegar Arms NP10 9AS
Tel: 01633 664999
B4591 Risca, left after r'bout

13. Handpost Hotel NP20 3EA
Tel: 01633 264502
B4591 Newport

M4 Jn 28

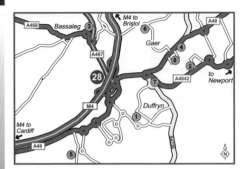

3. Junction 28 (Restaurant) NP10 8LD
Tel: 01633 891891
A467 North, at 2nd r'bout

4. **MCDONALD'S RESTAURANT**
NP20 3BA
Tel: 01633 215801
A48 North

5. Parc Golf Club NP10 8TU
Tel: 01633 680933
A48 South, left Church Lane

6. Spar NP20 3NA
Tel: 01633 266102
A48 North, left to Gaer, right Bassaleg Road

7. Stonehouse Brewers Fayre NP10 8TG
Tel: 01633 810541
A48 North, A4042, at 2nd r'bout

8. Tesco Supermarket NP20 3BA
Tel: 0845 677 9492
A48 North, on right

1. **ASDA** **ASDA NEWPORT**
NP10 8XL
Tel: 01633 815571
A48 South, left at 2nd r'bout, on left

2. ATS Euromaster Ltd NP20 2NN
Tel: 01633 216115
A48 North, A4042, on left

M4 Jn 30

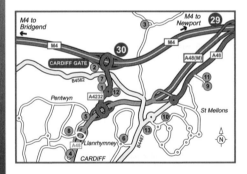

5. Hotel Campanile CF23 8HA
Tel: 029 20549044
A4232 South, A48 South

6. Ibis Hotel Cardiff Gate CF23 8RA
Tel: 029 20733222
At Cardiff Gate Services

7. **MCDONALD'S RESTAURANT**
CF23 8NL
Tel: 029 20733228
A4232 South, right at r'bout

8. Pentwyn Leisure Centre & Pool CF23 7EZ
Tel: 029 20549211
A48 South, on right

9. St. Mellon's Golf Club CF3 2XS
Tel: 01633 680401
A48 East, on right

10. Tesco Supermarket CF3 0EF
Tel: 0845 677 9598
A48 East, right at r'bout, left at r'bout

11. The St Mellons Hotel CF3 2XR
Tel: 01633 680355
A48 East, on right

12. The Unicorn Inn CF3 6YA
Tel: 029 20777185
A4232 South, left at r'bout

13. St Mellons Service Station CF3 5UG
Tel: 029 20777057
A48 East, right at r'bout, on left

1. **ASDA** **ASDA PENTWYN**
CF23 8NL
Tel: 029 20733853
A4232 South, on right

2. Cardiff Gate Restaurant CF23 8RD
Tel: 029 20541132
A4232 South, right St Mellons Rd

3. Cefn Mably Farm Park CF3 6XL
Tel: 029 20799923
A48 East, follow signs

4. Coed-Y-Gores Harvester Restaurant CF23 9PD
Tel: 029 20549866
A48 South

M4 Jn 32

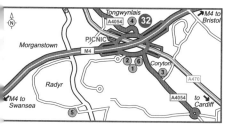

4. Quality Hotel (Cardiff) CF15 7LD
   Tel: 029 20529988
   North side of junction

5. Radyr Golf Club CF15 8BS
   Tel: 029 20842408
   A470 North, B4262 South, right Drysgol Rd, on left

6. Village Hotel & Leisure Club CF14 7EF
   Tel: 029 20524300
   A4054 South, on right

1. **ASDA** ASDA CARDIFF
   CF14 7EW
   Tel: 02920 613213
   On r'bout South of motorway

2. Esso Petrol Station CF14 7EW
   Tel: 029 20616044
   On r'bout South of motorway

3. Hollybush Inn Restaurant CF14 7EG
   Tel: 029 20625037
   A4054 South, on left

M4 Jn 34

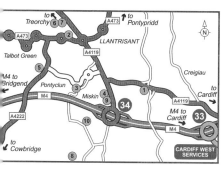

. Dynevor Arms CF72 8NS
   Tel: 029 20890530
   Follow A4119 East, on right.

2. **M** MCDONALD'S RESTAURANT
   CF72 8RP
   Tel: 01443 222859
   A4119 North, left A473

. Miskin Arms Pub & Restaurant CF72 8JQ
   Tel: 01443 224346
   A4119 North, 2nd set of lights, left into Miskin

4. Miskin Manor Hotel CF72 8ND
   Tel: 01443 224204
   A4119 Llantrisant, on left

5. The Pagoda Chinese Restaurant CF72 9DP
   Tel: 01443 224335
   A4119 North, left A473, left A4222

6. Somerfield Supermarket CF72 8LW
   Tel: 01443 226764
   A4119 North, on left

7. Tesco Supermarket & Petrol CF72 8RB
   Tel: 01443 617749
   A4119 North, on left

8. Vale Hotel & Golf Club CF72 8JY
   Tel: 01443 667800
   South from Junction, right Hensol, bear left

9. Woosters Restaurant CF72 8ND
   Tel: 01443 223883
   A4119 North, on left

10. Llanerch Vineyard Guest House CF72 8GG
    Tel: 01443 225877
    Signposted from Junction one mile South

M4 Jn 35

1. Cafe Petite Steak Restaurant CF35 5NG
Tel: 01656 862783
Follow signs for Pencoed, opposite petrol station

2. Coed Y Mwstwr Golf Club CF35 6AF
Tel: 01656 862121
A473 Bridgend, rt to Coychurch, rt at garage

3. Crossroads Services (Petrol) CF35 5HY
Tel: 01656 863686
North of junction

4. Forte Travelodge & Harvester Restaurant CF35 5HU
Tel: 01656 864404
A473 North, right at r'bout, left

5. Murco Petroleum Ltd CF35 5NH
Tel: 01656 863855
A473 North, left Felindre Rd, rt T-junction

6. Pencoed Balti CF35 5NW
Tel: 01656 862210
A473 North, left Felindre Rd, right, 2nd left

7. Pencoed Swimming Pool CF35 5PB
Tel: 01656 862360
A473 North, left Felindre Rd

8. The Star Inn CF35 5DL ♿
Tel: 01656 658458
A473 Bridgend, left at r'bout

9. Brewsters & Travel Inn CF35 5HY
Tel: 01656 864792
North of junction

M4 Jn 36

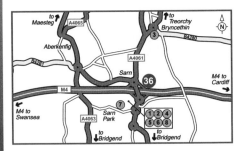

1. Harry Ramsdens CF32 9SU
Tel: 01656 653643
South of junction in Welsh Designer Outlet

2. KFC Restaurant CF32 9SU
Tel: 01656 669503
South of junction in Welsh Designer Outlet

3. Masons Arms Hotel CF32 9YR
Tel: 01656 720253
A4061 Bryncethin, on right ♿

4. Pizza Hut CF32 9SU
Tel: 01656 663500
South of junction in Welsh Designer Outlet

5. Sainsburys Supermarket CF32 9ST
Tel: 01656 648951
South of junction, on right

6. Sidoli Gelateria Capri (Restaurant) CF32 9SU
Tel: 01656 660568
South of junction in Welsh Designer Outlet

7. Costa Coffee CF32 9SU
Tel: 01656 645980
South of junction in Welsh Designer Outlet

8. **MCDONALD'S RESTAURANT CF32 9ST**
Tel: 01656 649415
A4061 South, right at r'bout

M4 Jn 37

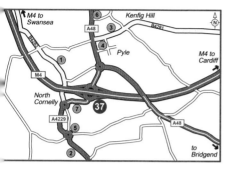

4. Pyle Swimming Pool CF33 6RP
   Tel: 01656 744019
   A48 North, B4281, rt Marshfield Av

5. South Cornelly Service Station CF33 4RE
   Tel: 01656 746658
   A4229 South

6. Texaco CF33 6HR
   Tel: 01656 747850
   A48 North

7. Ty Tanglwyst Farm Holiday Cottages CF33 4SA
   Tel: 01656 745635
   A4229, at r'bout North Cornelly Rd, on right

. Greenacre Public House & Hotel CF33 4LH
  Tel: 01656 743041
  North Cornelly, right to Heol Fach   ♿

. Grove Golf Club CF33 4RP
  Tel: 01656 788771
  A4229 South

. Mukta Mahal Tandoori CF33 6DA
  Tel: 01656 746000
  A48 North, B4281

M4 Jn 38/39

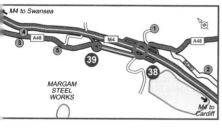

3. Mount Guest House SA13 1LR
   Tel: 01639 761077
   A48 Swansea, on left

4. Somerset Arms Hotel (Pub Restaurant) SA13 1LP
   Tel: 01639 887026
   A48 Swansea, on right

5. Twelve Knights Hotel SA13 2DB
   Tel: 01639 882381
   A48 Swansea, on left

. Abbotts Kitchen (Restaurant) SA13 2TA
  Tel: 01639 871184
  A48 South, first left

. Lakeside Golf Club & Driving Range SA13 2PA
  Tel: 01639 899959
  A48 South, B4283, on left

M4 Jn 40

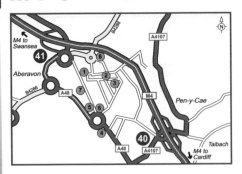

1. The Bistro SA13 1NU
   Tel: 01639 887390
   A48 North, right Station Rd, right Forge Rd

2. Forge Guest House SA13 1PF
   Tel: 01639 884416
   A48 North, right Station Rd, right Forge Rd

3. Oakwood SA13 1BD
   Tel: 01639 886627
   A48 North, rt Station Rd, rt Grove Pl, on left

4. Port Talbot Service Station SA13 1HN
   Tel: 01639 883418
   A48 North

5. Shah Tandoori SA13 1NN
   Tel: 01639 890131
   A48 North, right Station Rd

6. The Grand Hotel SA13 1DE
   Tel: 01639 882830
   A48 North, on right

7. Town Tyres Services SA13 1NW
   Tel: 01639 882281
   A48 North, right Station Rd

8. Tesco Supermarket SA13 1YA
   Tel: 0845 677 9562
   A48 N, rt 2nd r'bt, over next r'bt, at next r'bt

M4 Jn 41

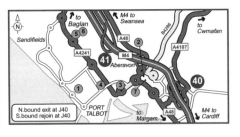

1. Aquadome & Afan Lido Leisure Complex SA12 6QW
   Tel: 01639 871444
   A4241, left at r'bout, left at bottom

2. Market Tavern SA13 1PB
   Tel: 01639 885292
   At r'bout by exit

3. **MCDONALD'S RESTAURANT**
   SA12 6LL
   Tel: 01639 870593
   B4286, at r'bout

4. Vivian Park Hotel Ltd SA12 6QG
   Tel: 01639 888311
   A4241, left Victoria Rd

5. ATS Euromaster Ltd SA12 6NR
   Tel: 01639 883895
   A4241 North

6. Morrisons Supermarket SA12 7BZ
   Tel: 01639 922097
   A4241 North

7. Tesco Supermarket SA13 1YA
   Tel: 0845 6779562
   Bear left at S/bound exit at r'bout

M4 Jn 42

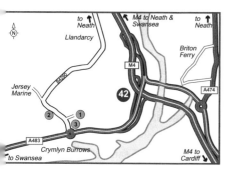

2. **The Towers Hotel** SA10 6JL
   Tel: 01792 814155
   A483 South, right at first r'bout, on left

3. **Shell Swansea Bay** SA10 6JN
   Tel: 01792 326900
   A483 Swansea, on right at r'bout

Swansea Bay Golf Club SA10 6JP
Tel: 01792 812198
A483 Swansea, right B4290, first right

M4 Jn 43

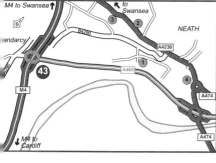

2. **Friends Café** SA10 6UT
   Tel: 01792 818383
   A465, A474 North, A4230 West, on right

3. **Maharaja Tandoori** SA10 6EW
   Tel: 01792 813705
   A465, A474 North, A4230 West, on left

4. **Tesco Supermarket** SA10 7FE
   Tel: 0845 6779484
   A465, A474 North, on left

Enterprise Tyres & Exhaust SA10 7DR
Tel: 01792 816731
A465, on left

M4 Jn 44

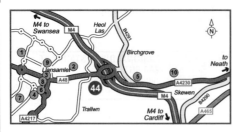

1. **ASDA** **ASDA SWANSEA SA6 8PS**
   Tel: 01792 763800
   A48 West, right at r'bout

2. D W M Petrol Station SA7 9BA
   Tel: 01792 775577
   A48 West

3. Dylan Thomas Restaurant SA7 9AQ
   Tel: 01792 701670
   A48 West

4. **halfords** **HALFORDS SA7 9EH**
   Tel: 01792 796601
   A48 West, lt A4217, rt Fendrod Way, lt Phoenix Way

5. Oaktree Parc Hotel & Restaurant Ltd SA7 9JR
   Tel: 01792 817781
   A4230 East

6. RAC Auto Windscreens SA7 9FD
   Tel: 01792 792723
   A48 West, left A4217

7. Ramada Jarvis SA7 9EG
   Tel: 01792 310330
   A48 West, lt A4217, rt Fendrod Way, lt Phoenix Way

8. Tesco Supermarket SA7 9RD
   Tel: 0845 677 9652
   A48 West, left A4217

9. The Plough & Harrow SA7 9RL
   Tel: 01792 772263
   A48 West, rt Llansamlet

10. Travellers Well SA10 6RG
    Tel: 01792 812002
    A4230 East

M4 Jn 45

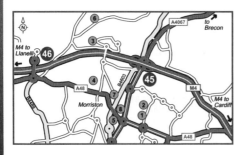

1. Brewsters & Travel Inn SA6 8WB
   Tel: 01792 311920
   A4067 South, left A48, left at r'bout

2. KFC Restaurant SA6 8PP
   Tel: 01792 700417
   A4067 South, left A48, left at r'bout

3. Morriston Leisure Centre (swimming pool) SA6 6NN
   Tel: 01792 797082
   B4603 South, imm right, right r'bout, left r'bout

4. Morriston Golf Club SA6 6AJ
   Tel: 01792 771079
   A4067 South, right at 2nd r'bout, on right

5. Somerfield Supermarket SA6 8AG
   Tel: 01792 774634
   At r'bout take B4603 South, on left

6. The Barn Inn & Restaurant SA6 6PX
   Tel: 01792 774411
   B4603 North, lt Quarr Dr, lt Heol Dywyll, on right

7. The Red Lion Hotel SA6 6JA
   Tel: 01792 773206
   B4603 South, on right

8. **McDONALD'S RESTAURANT SA6 8DU**
   Tel: 01792 774295
   A4067 South, off on right

M4 Jn 47

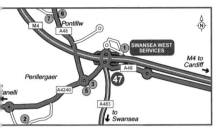

Travelodge SA4 1GT
Tel: 0870 1911555
At services

Busy Lizzies Café SA4 1WF
Tel: 01792 894062
A4240, left at lights, on left

3. Cross Service Station SA4 9AQ
Tel: 01792 222932
A4240, left at r'bout

---

4. **MCDONALD'S RESTAURANT**
SA4 9GT
Tel: 01792 898655
At services

---

5. Old Inn (Restaurant) SA4 9AQ
Tel: 01792 894097
A4240, at r'bout

6. Pontlliw Service Station SA4 9EF
Tel: 01792 892020
A48, in Pontlliw

7. The Buck Inn (Pub Restaurant) SA4 9EF
Tel: 01792 892294
A48, in Pontlliw

M4 Jn 48

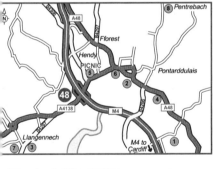

Alltygraban Golf Club SA4 9DT
Tel: 01792 885757
A48 South, right Allt-Y-Graban Road

Co-op Supermarket SA4 8ST
Tel: 01792 882212
A48 South, on right

3. Co-op Foodstore SA14 8TS
Tel: 01554 820202
A4138, B4297, on left

4. Fountain Inn SA4 8JP
Tel: 01792 882501
A48 South, on right

5. Spar Supermarket SA4 0XE
Tel: 01792 884312
North at junction, on left

6. The Gwyn Hotel SA4 8TH
Tel: 01792 882187
A48 South, on right

7. The Old Bridge Inn & Restaurant SA14 8TW
Tel: 01554 821301
A4138, B4297, on right

8. White Springs Fishery SA4 8QG
Tel: 01792 885699
A48 into P/dulais, follow Lye Ind Est, on right

DON'T DRIVE TIRED.

THINK!

Make Time For A Bre

M5 Summary

🛏️🍵✕🛒🍷 **14**	**Wotton-u-Edge, B4509** .... *Page 62*	
	7 miles	
No Accessible Facilities **15**	**M4**	
	1 mile	
🛏️🍵✕🔧🛒🛒🍷 **16**	**Thornbury A38** .... *Page 63*	
	2 miles	
Ⓜ️ **ASDA** *Harry Ramsden's* **halfords** 🛏️🍵✕🔧🛒(TTD)🛒🍷 **17**	**Bristol A4018** .... *Page 63*	
	4 miles	
🛏️🍵✕🔧🛒🛒🍷 **18**	**Avonmouth A4** .... *Page 64*	
	2 miles	
🛏️🍵✕🛒🍷 **19**	**Portishead A369** .... *Page 64* **Gordano Services**	
	7 miles	
🍵✕🔧🛒🛒🍷 **20**	**Nailsea, Clevedon B3133** .... *Page 65*	
	6 miles	
Kwik-Fit 🍵✕🔧🛒🛒🍷 **21**	**Weston-Super-Mare A370** .... *Page 65*	
	6 miles	
⚫	**Sedgemoor Services**	
	4 miles	
🛏️🍵✕🛒🍷 **22**	**Weston-Super-Mare A38** .... *Page 66*	
	5 miles	
halfords 🛏️🍵✕🔧🛒🛒🍷 **23**	**Bridgwater A38** .... *Page 66*	
	5 miles	
🛏️🍵✕🛒🍷 **24**	**Minehead A38** .... *Page 67* **Bridgewater Services**	
	7 miles	
Ⓜ️ **ASDA halfords** 🔧🛏️🍵✕(TTD)🛒🍷 **25**	**Taunton A358** .... *Page 67*	
	5 miles	
⚫	**Taunton Deane Services**	
	2 miles	
🍵✕🛒🍷 **26**	**Wellington A38** .... *Page 68*	
	8 miles	
🛏️🍵✕🛒(TTD)🍷 **27**	**Tiverton A361** .... *Page 68*	
	4 miles	
Ⓜ️ 🛏️🍵✕🛒(TTD)🛒🍷 **28**	**Cullompton B3181, A373** ..... *Page 69*	
	10 miles	
No Facilities Listed **29**	**Honiton A30**	
	1 mile	
🛏️🍵✕🔧(TTD)🛒🍷 **30**	**Exeter A379** .... *Page 69* **Exeter Services**	
	4 miles	
No Facilities Listed **31**	**Bodmin A30**	
	Total Dist. = 90 miles	

NORTH

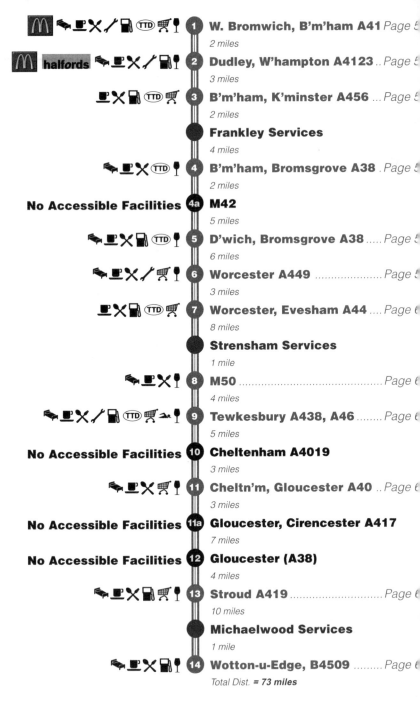

🅜 🛏☕✕🔧⛽(TTD)🛒🍷	**1**	W. Bromwich, B'm'ham A41 *Page 5*
		2 miles
🅜 **halfords** 🛏☕✕🔧⛽🍷	**2**	Dudley, W'hampton A4123 .. *Page 5*
		3 miles
☕✕⛽(TTD)🛒	**3**	B'm'ham, K'minster A456 ... *Page 5*
		2 miles
⬤		**Frankley Services**
		4 miles
🛏☕✕(TTD)🍷	**4**	B'm'ham, Bromsgrove A38 . *Page 5*
		2 miles
No Accessible Facilities	**4a**	**M42**
		5 miles
🛏☕✕⛽(TTD)🍷	**5**	D'wich, Bromsgrove A38 ..... *Page 5*
		6 miles
🛏☕✕🔧🛒🍷	**6**	Worcester A449 .... *Page 5*
		3 miles
☕✕⛽(TTD)🛒	**7**	Worcester, Evesham A44 .... *Page 6*
		8 miles
⬤		**Strensham Services**
		1 mile
🛏☕✕🍷	**8**	M50 .... *Page 6*
		4 miles
🛏☕✕🔧⛽(TTD)🛒🍸🍷	**9**	Tewkesbury A438, A46 .... *Page 6*
		5 miles
No Accessible Facilities	**10**	Cheltenham A4019
		3 miles
🛏☕✕🛒🍷	**11**	Cheltn'm, Gloucester A40 .. *Page 6*
		3 miles
No Accessible Facilities	**11a**	Gloucester, Cirencester A417
		7 miles
No Accessible Facilities	**12**	Gloucester (A38)
		4 miles
🛏☕✕⛽🛒🍷	**13**	Stroud A419 .... *Page 6*
		10 miles
⬤		**Michaelwood Services**
		1 mile
🛏☕✕⛽🍷	**14**	Wotton-u-Edge, B4509 .... *Page 6*
		Total Dist. **= 73 miles**

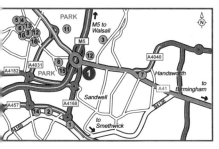

ATS Euromaster Ltd B66 1HJ
Tel: 0121 565 0179
A4168 South, at 2nd r'bout

Desi 2 Public House B66 1HX
Tel: 0121 565 2694
A4168, right A457

Hilltop Golf Course B21 8LJ
Tel: 0121 554 4463
A41 East, 1st left after W/Bromwich FC

KFC Restaurant B70 8ND
Tel: 0121 553 2119
A41 West, left at r'bout

La Casa Greek Restaurant B70 8AQ
Tel: 0121 553 4893
A41 West, left at r'bout

6.	MCDONALD'S RESTAURANT B70 7QG Tel: 0121 553 0436 📇 🚻 ♿ ✕ ⊘
A41 West, left at r'bout	

M5 Jn 2

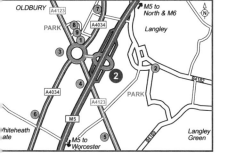

Birchley Park Service Station B69 2BD
Tel: 0121 552 6957
At main r'bout

Crosswells Inn B69 4SB   ♿
Tel: 0121 552 2629
A4034 North, right to Langley, right B4182

7.	MCDONALD'S RESTAURANT B21 0AP Tel: 0121 525 2885 📇 🚻 ♿ ✕ ⊘
A41 East	

8. Mibsons Service Station B70 6QG
Tel: 0121 525 4100
1st exit (N/bound), on left   ♿

9. Pizza Hut B70 7QU
Tel: 0121 500 5232
A41 West, left at r'bout

10. Safeway Supermarket B70 7QU
Tel: 0121 500 5106
A41 West, left at r'bout

11. Sandwell Valley Country Park B71 4BG
Tel: 0121 553 0220
A41 West, follow signs Sandwell Park Farm

12. Shalimar Restaurant B70 6NY
Tel: 0121 553 1319
A41 West, left at r'bout

13. Tesco Supermarket B70 7NH
Tel: 0845 677 9709
A41 West, left at r'bout

14. The Full Montea Café B66 1JG
Tel: 0121 558 4842
A4618 Smethwick, right at 2nd r'bout, on left

15. The Vine B70 6RD
Tel: 0121 553 2866
Follow sign to W/Browich Town Centre, rt, on lt

16. Days Hotel B70 6JJ
Tel: 0121 525 8333
A41 West, left at r'bout

3.	HALFORDS B69 1DT Tel: 0121 552 6173 🔧
At main r'bout	

4.	MCDONALD'S RESTAURANT B69 4RJ Tel: 0121 541 2055 📇 🚻 ♿ ✕ ⊘
Left at main r'bout	

5. Saffron Indian Restaurant B69 4RR
Tel: 0121 552 1752
A4123 South, on right

6. The Bulls Head B69 1AQ
Tel: 0121 559 2637
A4034 South

7. The Manchester Stores (Public House) B69 2AS
Tel: 0121 552 2556
A4034 North

8. The One & Two Halves B69 2AQ   ♿
Tel: 0121 544 9621
5th exit at r'bt, slip road behind petrol station

9. Express By Holiday Inn B69 2BD
Tel: 0121 511 0000
At main r'bout

M5 Jn 3

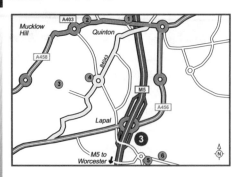

3. Halesowen Golf Club B62 8QF
Tel: 0121 501 3606
A456 East, lt at 2nd r'bout, lt Spies Ln, rt Leasowes Ln

4. Co-op Supermarket B62 8PY
Tel: 0121 422 2294
A456 East, lt at 2nd r'bout, lt Spies Ln, at r'bout

5. Woodgate Service Station B32 3QU
Tel: 0121 422 3239
A456 West, first left, over r'bout

6. Woodgate Valley Country Park B32 3DS
Tel: 0121 421 7575
A456 Kidderminster, 1st left, Close Lane, Clapgate Lane

1. Co-op Supermarket B62 9AS
Tel: 0121 422 0003
A456 East, left at 2nd r'bout, on right

2. Dilshad Indian Restaurant B62 9AA
Tel: 0121 421 6549
A456 East, left at 2nd r'bout, on right

M5 Jn 4

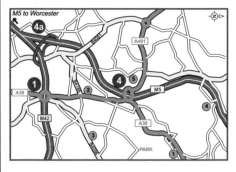

3. Honeypot Guest House B60 1HQ
Tel: 0121 445 2580
A38 South, lt to Braces Ln, on left in Old Bmngm Rd

4. Waseley Hills Country Park B45 9AT
Tel: 01562 710025
A491, Signposted from junction

5. WILDMOOR OAK PUB RESTAURANT B61 0RE
Tel: 0121 453 2696
Good homemade food seven days a week
A491 West, left into Top Rd, on left

1. Banophool Balti Tandoori Cuisine B45 9HY
Tel: 0121 457 9358
A38 North, on right

2. Hilton (Bromsgrove) B61 0JB
Tel: 0121 447 4588
A38 South, on right

M5 Jn 5

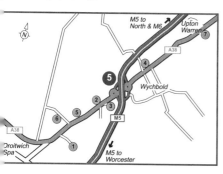

- Chateau Impney WR9 0BN
  Tel: 01905 774411
  A38 South, on left

- Little Chef WR9 0BS
  Tel: 01527 861594
  A38 South, on right

3. The Robin Hood (Pub & Restaurant) WR9 0BS
   Tel: 01527 861931
   A38 South, on left

4. The Poachers Pocket (Pub & Restaurant) WR9 7PE
   Tel: 01905 458615
   A38 North, on left

5. Travelodge WR9 0BJ
   Tel: 0870 191 1574
   A38 South, on right

6. Droitwich Golf & Country Club WR9 0BQ
   Tel: 01905 774344
   A38 South, right Ford Land

7. Swan Service Station B61 7ES
   Tel: 01527 861892
   A38 North, on right

M5 Jn 6

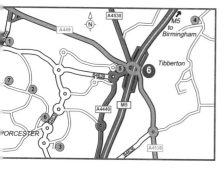

- Mobile Windscreen Ltd WR4 9XN
  Tel: 01905 755455
  B4639, on right

- Spar Shop WR4 9PA
  Tel: 01905 755021
  B4639, left Cranham Drive, on left

3. Tesco Supermarket WR4 0UJ
   Tel: 01905 877445
   B4639, left at r'bout, left at 4th r'bout, on right

4. The Bridge Inn WR9 7NQ
   Tel: 01905 345874
   A4538 Evesham, signposted Tibberton

5. Travel Inn & Beefeater Restaurant WR4 9FA
   Tel: 0870 197 7278
   A4440, at junction

6. Wyvern Windscreens WR4 0JN
   Tel: 01905 724204
   B4639, left at r'bout, on right (B4638)

7. Sainsbury's Supermarket WR4 9JN
   Tel: 01905 754747
   B4639, left at T-junction, left at r'bout, on left

M5 Jn 7

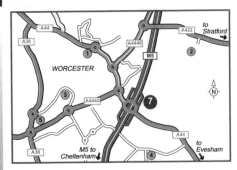

3. Tesco Supermarket WR5 3SW
Tel: 0845 677 9738
A4440 West, right at r'bout, on left

4. The Retreat Restaurant WR5 2PT
Tel: 01905 820274
A44 Evesham, right Woodbury Ln, on left

5. The Timberdine Harvester (Retaurant) WR5 3HP
Tel: 01905 359294
A4440 West, right at 2nd r'bout, on right

1. Rottner & Rudge Petrol Station WR5 2JY
Tel: 01905 351245
A44 West, on left at 3rd r'bout

2. SPETCHLEY GARDENS WR5 1RS
Tel: 01453 810303
Relax in a 30 acre garden oasis • Tea room
A44 West, A4440 North, A422 East, on right

M5 Jn 8

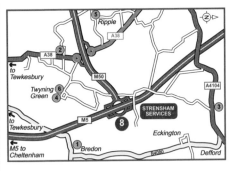

3. Pio's Restaurant Ltd WR8 9BW
Tel: 01386 750327
M50, A38 North, A4104 East, on left

4. The Fleet Inn GL20 6FL
Tel: 01684 274310
At M50 J1 take Brockridge Rd to Fleet Ln

5. The Railway Inn GL20 6EY
Tel: 01684 592225
M50, A38 Worcester, left to Ripple

6. Village Inn The GL20 6DF
Tel: 01684 293500
At M50 J1 take Brockridge Rd to Village Inn

1. Fox & Hounds Inn GL20 7LA
Tel: 01684 772377
M50, A38 South, left on B4080, on left

2. Hilton Hotel Puckrup Hall GL20 6EL
Tel: 01684 296200
M50, A38, first right, on left

M5 Jn 9

. ATS Euromaster Ltd GL20 5LU
  Tel: 01684 292461
  A438 West, right at r'bout

2. Cascades Leisure Centre & Pool GL20 5LR
   Tel: 01684 293740
   A438 West, right at r'bout

3. Croft Farm Leisure And Water Park GL20 7EE
   Tel: 01684 772321
   A438 West, right at r'bout, right B4080

4. Little Chef GL20 8JN
   Tel: 01684 850270
   A46 East

5. My Great Grandfathers (Restaurant) GL20 5RX
   Tel: 01684 292687
   A438 West, left at r'bout

6. Rajshahi GL20 5JU
   Tel: 01684 273727
   A438 Tewkesbury, High Street

7. Rottner & Rudge Petrol Station GL20 8DT
   Tel: 01684 297583
   A438 West

8. Royal Hop Pole GL20 5RT
   Tel: 01684 293236
   A438 West, left at r'bout

9. Safeway Supermarket GL20 8AB
   Tel: 01684 273261
   A438 West

10. Spa Villa Guest House GL20 8DS
    Tel: 01684 292487
    A438 Tewkesbury, on left

11. Tesco Supermarket GL20 5LQ
    Tel: 0845 677 9670
    A438 West, right at r'bout

12. The Great Wall Chinese Restaurant GL20 5AL
    Tel: 01684 292046
    A438 West, right at r'bout

13. Tudor House Hotel GL20 5BH
    Tel: 01684 297755
    A438 West, right at r'bout

14. BP Petrol Station GL20 8JN
    Tel: 01684 293785
    A46 East

M5 Jn 11

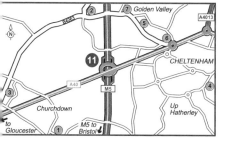

. Bat & Ball Inn GL3 2ER
  Tel: 01452 713172
  A40 Glouc, left at lights, on left

. Hope Orchard Guest House GL51 0TF
  Tel: 01452 855556
  A40 Cheltenham, left B4063, on right

3. Somerfield Supermarket GL3 2BX
   Tel: 01452 713011
   A40 Glouc, right at r'bout(B4063), 1st rt, 1st lt

4. Spar GL51 3JA
   Tel: 01242 525100
   A40 Chelt, rt r'bt, lt r'bt, lt r'bt, rt T-Junc

5. The Pheasant Inn (Pub Restaurant) GL51 0SS
   Tel: 01452 713246
   A40 Cheltenham, left at r'bout, on right

6. Thistle Hotel (Cheltenham) GL51 0TS
   Tel: 01242 232691
   A40 Cheltenham, on left at r'bout

7. The White House Hotel GL51 0SS
   Tel: 01452 713226
   A40 Cheltenham, left at r'bout, on right

M5 Jn 13

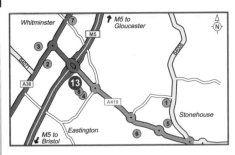

1. BP Service Station GL10 2PB
Tel: 01453 821005
A419 South, left at 2nd r'bout, right at T-junction

2. Fromebridge Self Serve GL2 7PG
Tel: 01452 740753
A419 North, left A38

3. Fromebridge Mill GL2 7PD
Tel: 01452 741796
A419 North, left A38, 1st right

4. Little Chef GL10 3SQ
Tel: 01453 828847
A419 South

5. Co-op Supermarket GL10 2NA
Tel: 01453 824348
A419 South, left at 2nd r'bout, right at T-junction

6. Stonehouse Court Hotel GL10 3RA
Tel: 01453 825155
A419 South

7. The Old Forge (Pub Restaurant) GL2 7NY
Tel: 01452 741306
A419 North, right A38

8. Travelodge GL10 3SQ
Tel: 0870 1911554
A419 South

M5 Jn 14

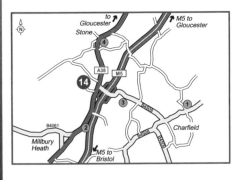

1. Charfield Service Station GL12 8SR
Tel: 01453 521384
B4509, left B4508, on left

2. The Park Hotel GL12 8DR
Tel: 01454 260550
A38 Bristol, on left

3. Tortworth Court Four Pillars Hotel GL12 8HH
Tel: 01454 263000
B4509, on right   &

4. The Elms at Stone (Hotel) GL13 9JX
Tel: 01454-260279
A38 Gloucester, in Stone

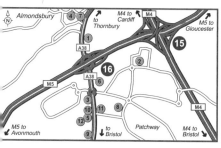

- Almondsbury Interchange Hotel BS32 4AA
  Tel: 01454 613206
  A38 North

- Autoglass BS32 4EU
  Tel: 01454 620900
  A38 South, left at r'bout, left at r'bout

- Aztec Hotel BS32 4TS
  Tel: 01454 201090
  A38 South

- Bowl Inn & Lilies Restaurant BS32 4DT
  Tel: 01454 612757
  A38 North, left 'The Scop', left Church Rd

5. Britannia Café BS34 6ND
Tel: 0117 979 8588
A38 South, on right

6. Hilton Hotels BS32 4JF
Tel: 01454 201144
A38 South, on left

7. Rocklands Restaurant BS32 4HD
Tel: 01454 612208
A38 North, left 'The Scop', on left

8. Somerfield BS32 9DA
Tel: 01454 617727
A38 South, left at r'bout, right at r'bout

9. Star Service Stations BS34 6NA
Tel: 01454 453000
A38 Bristol, on right

10. The Rookery Guest House BS34 6ND
Tel: 01454 850088
A38 South

11. Travellers Rest Hungry Horse (Pub Restaurant) BS34 6NR
Tel: 01454 612238
A38 South, on left

12. The Willow Court Lodge Hotel BS34 6ND
Tel: 01454 612276
A38 South

M5 Jn 17

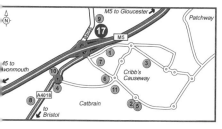

1. **ASDA** ASDA PATCHWAY
BS34 5TL
Tel: 0117 3172400
Take Highwood Lane at r'bout

- Burger King BS10 7SR
  Tel: 0117 959 0712
  Merlin Rd exit at r'bout

3. **halfords** HALFORDS
BS34 5TS
Tel: 0117 950 0230
Take Highwood Lane at r'bout

4. HARRY RAMSDENS
BS10 7TQ
Tel: 0117 959 4100
10% off bill on production of this book
A4018 South, 1st left, Lysander Road

5. KFC Restaurant BS10 7SR
Tel: 0117 959 1492
Merlin Rd exit at r'bout

6. **MCDONALD'S RESTAURANT
BS10 7UA**
Tel: 0117 950 1523
At junction take Merlin Rd

7. Morrisons Supermarket BS10 7UD
Tel: 0117 950 9103
Merlin Rd exit at r'bout

8. Shell Petrol Station Cribbs Causeway BS10 7TG
Tel: 0117 941 9400
A4018, 1 mile on right.

9. The Bristol Golf Club BS10 7TP
Tel: 01454 620000
Exit to Severn Beach B4055, on right

10. Travelodge & Harvester Restaurant BS10 7TL
Tel: 0870 191 1721
A4018, at r'bout

11. Bella Italia Restaurant BS10 7SR
Tel: 0117 959 0982
Merlin Rd exit at r'bout

M5 Jn 18

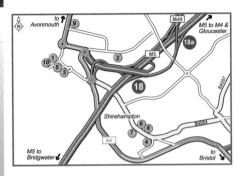

1. Andels Cafe BS11 9AA
Tel: 0117 908 1105
Head for Avonmouth Village, Gloucester Rd

2. ATS Euromaster Ltd BS11 8DG
Tel: 0117 982 4706
A4 North, right at r'bout

3. Avonmouth Guesthouse BS11 9EL
Tel: 0117 982 2646
A4 North, left at r'bout

4. Maharajas Restaurant BS11 9TU
Tel: 0117 982 0213
A4 South, left B4054, right turn

5. Portview Hotel BS11 9JB
Tel: 0117 982 8030
A4 North, left at r'bout

6. Shirehampton Lodge Hotel BS11 0DJ
Tel: 0117 907 3480
A4 South, left B4054

7. Shirehampton Service Station BS11 0DE
Tel: 0117 937 9040
A4 South, left B4054

8. Somerfield Supermarket BS11 0DJ
Tel: 0117 982 3376
A4 South, left B4054

9. St Andrews Service Station BS11 9HS
Tel: 0117 987 2840
A4 North

10. The Royal Hotel BS11 9AD
Tel: 0117 982 2847
Avonmouth Village, Gloucester Rd

M5 Jn 19

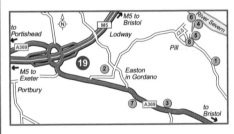

1. Glendale Bed & Breakfast BS20 0HA
Tel: 01275 373130
A369 S, lt St George's Hill, over crossrds, on lt

2. KINGS ARMS BS20 0PS
Tel: 01275 372208
Quality home cooked food, real ales
A369 Easton, 1st left, on left

3. Markham Filling Station BS20 0QH
Tel: 01275 372122
A369 Bristol, on main road

4. Riverside Guest House BS20 0EN
Tel: 01275 374629
A369 S, 1st lt, lt Mt Pleasant, on rt W/House Rd

5. The Arches Guest House BS20 0AQ
Tel: 01275 373194
A369 S, 1st lt, lt Pill St, on lt, Bank Pl

6. The Duke Of Cornwall BS20 0BG
Tel: 01275 371237
A369 Bristol, left to Village, left after shops

7. The Tynings B&B BS20 0QE
Tel: 01275 372608
A369 Bristol, half mile on right

8. World Of Spice Tandoori BS20 0EL
Tel: 01275 371111
A369 S, 1st left, left Pill St

M5 Jn 20

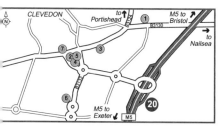

. Clevedon Service Station BS21 6AB
Tel: 01275 343081
Right at r'bout, left at T-junction, on right

. The Grapevine Wine Bar & Bistro BS21 6NH
Tel: 01275 873150
1st right after 2 r'bouts ♿

. Hi-Q Tyre Services BS21 6DL
Tel: 01275 874721
Right at 2nd r'bout, right at crossroads on right

4. Safeway Supermarket BS21 6HX
Tel: 01275 876671
Over 2nd r'bout, on right

5. Tandoori Nights BS21 6HX
Tel: 01275 342342
Over 2nd r'bout, on right

6. Tesco Supermarket BS21 6LH
Tel: 0845 677 9165
Left at 2nd r'bout, on right

7. Mr Beans Café BS21 6LY
Tel: 01275 873222
Straight over 2 r'bouts

M5 Jn 21

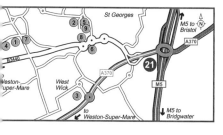

. Co-op Supermarket BS22 6JD
Tel: 01934 514257
A370 West, right B3440, right High St

2. **Kwik-Fit** // **KWIK-FIT**
   BS22 6BX
   Tel: 01934 514777
   A370 West, right B3440, right Queens Wy 🔧

. Safeway Supermarket BS24 7AY
Tel: 01934 517883
On A370 West

. Somerfield Supermarket BS22 6HG
Tel: 01934 513959
A370 West, right B3440, right High St

5. The Parish Pump (Public House) BS22 6BT
Tel: 01934 512046
A370 West, right B3440, North Worle Shop Ctr ♿

6. The Summerhouse (Pub Restaurant) BS22 6WE
Tel: 01934 520011
A370 West, right B3440

7. The Woodspring (Pub Restaurant) BS22 6JJ
Tel: 01934 510505
A370 West, right B3440, right High St

8. Petrol Station BS22 6BQ
Tel: 01934 511414
A370 West, right B3440, at r'bout

9. Sainsbury's Supermarket BS22 6BL
Tel: 01934 510495
A370 West, right B3440, North Worle Shop Ctr

M5 Jn 22

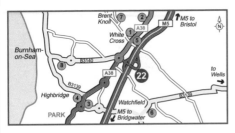

1. Battleborough Grange Country Hotel TA9 4HJ
   Tel: 01278 760208
   On A38 North

2. Brent House Restaurant TA9 4HL
   Tel: 01278 760246
   On A38 North

3. George Hotel TA9 3AE
   Tel: 01278 783248
   On A38 South

4. Highbridge Tandoori TA9 3HR
   Tel: 01278 782560
   On A38 South

5. The Goathouse Restaurant TA9 4HJ
   Tel: 01278 760995
   On A38 North &

6. Watchfield Inn (Pub Restaurant) TA9 4RD
   Tel: 01278 783551
   A38 South, left Burnham Moor Lane, right B3139

7. Woodlands Country House Hotel & Restaurant TA9 4D
   Tel: 01278 760232
   A38 North, left Brent Knoll, right follow signs

8. Tesco Supermarket TA8 1RA
   Tel: 0845 677 9089
   On B3140

M5 Jn 23

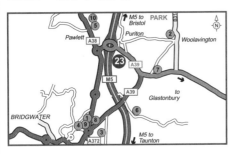

1. Bridgwater Self Serve (Petrol) TA6 4AZ
   Tel: 01278 424018
   A38 South

2. Chestnut House Hotel TA7 8EF
   Tel: 01278 683658
   A39 Glastonbury, left B3141

3. Costcutter Supermarket TA6 4RA &
   Tel: 01278 424555
   A39 Glastonbury, right under motorway, 2nd left

4. **halfords** **HALFORDS**
   TA6 4AE
   Tel: 01278 422166
   A38 South, right at r'bout

5. Hilltops Café TA6 4RT
   Tel: 01278 683716
   A38 Pawlett, top of hill &

6. J Denning Guest House TA7 8QR
   Tel: 01278 423201
   A39 Bridgwater, left Chedzoy Lane

7. Knowle Inn TA7 8PN
   Tel: 01278 685193
   A39 Glastonbury

8. Newmarket Hotel TA6 4PN
   Tel: 01278 422178
   A38 South, left A39

9. Sainsburys Supermarket TA6 4AB
   Tel: 01278 444066
   A38 South, right at r'bout

10. Warwick Filling Station TA6 4RT
    Tel: 01278 683348
    A38 North

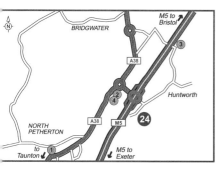

2. Grahams Transport Stop TA6 6PR
   Tel: 01278 663052
   A38 Taunton, on left

3. The Boat & Anchor TA7 0AQ
   Tel: 01278 662473
   A38 Bridgewater, rt at r'bout, lt at T-junc, on lt

4. Woods Service Station TA6 6PR
   Tel: 01278-663076
   A38 Taunton, on left

. Best Western Walnut Tree Hotel TA6 6QA
  Tel: 01278 662255
  A38 Taunton, on right

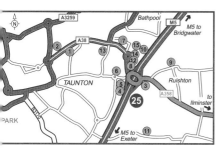

7. **MCDONALD'S RESTAURANT**
   TA1 2LP
   Tel: 01823 443765
   A38 West

8. Pizza Hut TA1 2LR
   Tel: 01823 444747
   A38 West

9. Ruishton Inn TA3 5JW
   Tel: 01823 442285
   A358, left after Blackbrook Tavern

10. Sainsburys Supermarket & Petrol Station TA1 2LP
    Tel: 01823 443163
    A38 West

11. Swingrite Golf Centre TA3 5AB
    Tel: 01823 442600
    A358 to Ilminster, 1st rt, rt at T-junc, 1st rt.

12. The Hankridge Arms (Pub Restaurant) TA1 2LR
    Tel: 01823 444405
    A358 Taunton, on right

13. Travel Inn & Beefeater Restaurant TA1 2DU
    Tel: 0870 197 7249
    A38 West, left Bridgewater Rd

14. Travelodge TA1 2LR
    Tel: 01823 444702
    A38 West

1. **ASDA** **ASDA TAUNTON**
   TA1 2AN
   Tel: 01823 252701
   A38 West

. Autoglass TA1 2AL
  Tel: 01823 270471
  A38 West

. Blackbrook Tavern TA3 5LU
  Tel: 01823 443121
  A358 Ruishton, on right

. Express By Holiday Inn TA1 2PX
  Tel: 01823 624000
  West of junction, immediate left

. Harvester Restaurants TA1 2PF
  Tel: 01823 442221
  West of junction, immediate left

. Holiday Inn TA1 2UA
  Tel: 0870 400 9080
  West of junction

15. **halfords** **HALFORDS**
    TA1 2LR
    Tel: 01823 443415
    A38 West

M5 Jn 26

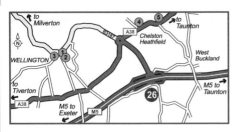

3. New Canton Chinese Restaurant TA21 8NS
Tel: 01823 666662
A38, B3187, left South Street

4. Piccadilly Filling Station TA21 9HY
01823 661469
A38 Taunton, on left

5. Blackbird Inn TA21 9HX
A38 Taunton, on left

1. Cafe Noir TA21 8NR
Tel: 01823 665264
A38, B3187, left South Street, on left

2. Green Dragon Inn TA21 8NR
Tel: 01823 662281
Wellington, left at lights in centre, on left

M5 Jn 27

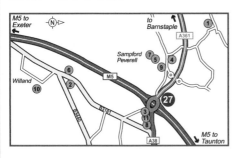

1. Brambles Guest House Bed And Breakfast EX16 7DS
Tel: 01884 829211
A361W, exit thru Samford P, over A361, to Whitnage

2. Culm Vale Filling Station EX15 2RF
Tel: 01884 820355
A38, first right, right at junction B3181

3. Little Chef EX16 7HD
Tel: 01884 821205
At junction on A38

4. Parkway House Country Hotel EX16 7BJ
Tel: 01884 820255
A361, exit Sampford Peverell

5. The Globe (Pub Restaurant) EX16 7BJ
Tel: 01884 821214
A361, exit Sampford Peverell

6. The Halfway House (Pub Restaurant) EX15 2RF
Tel: 01884 820258
B3181 Willand, 2 miles on right

7. The Merriemeade (Pub Restaurant) EX16 7BJ
Tel: 01884 820270
A361, exit Sampford Peverell

8. The Waterloo Cross Inn EX15 3ES
Tel: 01884 840328
On A38

9. Tiverton Parkway Golf Driving Range EX16 7EH
Tel: 01884 820825
A361, exit left

10. Weir Mill Farm (Guest House) EX15 2RE
Tel: 01884 820803
A38, first right, right B3181, in Willand

11. Shell Petrol Station EX16 7EJ
At junction on A38

M5 Jn 28

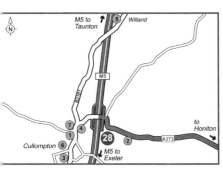

3. Padbrook Park Golf & Leisure Club EX15 1RU
Tel: 01884 34344
B3181 South

4. The Kings Head EX15 1AF
Tel: 01884 32418
B3181 South

5. Willand Service Station EX15 2PF
Tel: 01884 32282
B3181 North

6. Somerfield Supermarket EX15 1EY
Tel: 01884 32958
B3181 South

7. China Orchids Restaurant EX15 1AA
Tel: 01884 33336
B3181 South

1. Manor House Hotel EX15 1JL
Tel: 01884 32281
Exit West, B3181 South

2. **MCDONALD'S RESTAURANT EX15 1PA**
Tel: 01884 33678
A373 East

M5 Jn 30

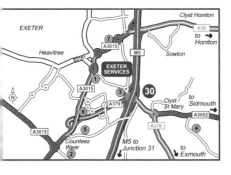

3. Mid Devon Tyres EX2 7JH
Tel: 01392 214101
Sidmouth Rd West

4. Old Mill House (Guest House) EX5 1AG
Tel: 01392 877733
Clyst St Mary, after r'bout 2nd right

5. Plantsmans Café & St. Bridget's Garden Ctr EX2 7JY
Tel: 01392 879234
A379, left Old Rydon Lane, on left

6. Tesco Supermarket EX2 7EZ
Tel: 0845 677 9263
A379, on right (double back)

7. The Barn Owl EX1 3PE
Tel: 01392 449011
West from junction, past services, left A3015

1. Exeter Arms Hotel EX2 7HL
Tel: 01392 435353
Sidmouth Rd West, left at r'bout, on left

2. Exeter Golf & Country Club EX2 7AE
Tel: 01392 874139
A379, left at r'bout, on left

M6 Summary

Stafford Services
4 miles

halfords 🛌🅿️✕🔧⛽ **14** **Stafford A34** ....*Page 7*
5 miles

🛌⛽🛒🍷 **13** **Stafford A449** ....*Page 7*
6 miles

🛌🅿️✕🛒🍷 **12** **Cannock, Telford A5** ....*Page 7*
2 miles

No Accessible Facilities **11a** **M6 Toll**
1 mile

🛌🅿️✕⛽🍷 **11** **Wolverhampton A460** ....*Page 7*
1 mile

Hilton Park Services
0 miles

No Accessible Facilities **10a** **M54**
6 miles

Ⓜ 🛌🅿️✕🔧⛽ **10** **Walsall A454** ....*Page 7*
1 mile

Ⓜ halfords 🛌🅿️✕🔧⛽🛒🍷 **9** **Wednesbury A461** ....*Page 7*
3 miles

No Accessible Facilities **8** **M5**
1 mile

ASDA 🛌🅿️✕🔧⛽🛒🍷 **7** **Walsall A34** ....*Page 7*
5 miles

🛌🅿️✕🔧⛽🍷 **6** **Birmingham A38** ....*Page 7*
3 miles

No Accessible Facilities **5** **Sutton Coldfield A452**
6 miles

No Accessible Facilities **4a** **M42**
3 miles

🛌🅿️✕⛽🍷 **4** **Coleshill A446** ....*Page 7*
6 miles

Corley Services
3 miles

🛌🅿️✕🔧🍷 **3** **Coventry A444** ....*Page 7*
3 miles

ASDA 🛌🅿️✕⛽ ⓉⓉⒹ 🛒🍷 **2** **Coventry A46** ....*Page 7*
8 miles

🛌🅿️✕⛽🛒🍷 **1** **Rugby A426** ....*Page 7*
Dist. = 67 miles

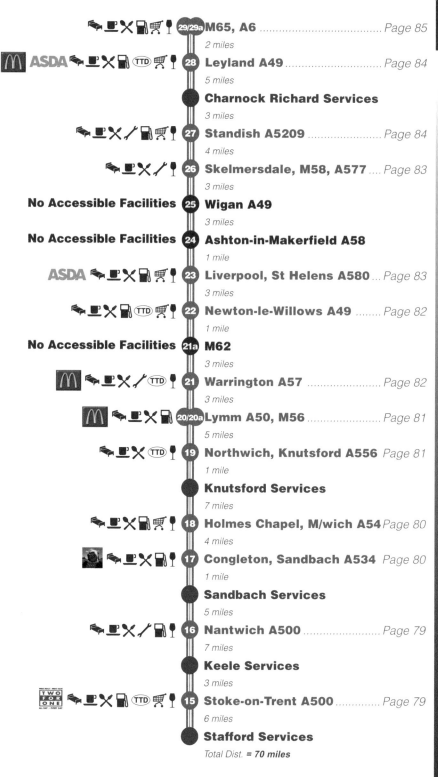

🛏️💺✕🔧📱🛒🍷	**29/29a**	**M65, A6**	*Page 85*
		2 miles	
🅼 **ASDA** 🛏️💺✕🔧 TTD 🛒🍷	**28**	**Leyland A49**	*Page 84*
		5 miles	
	●	**Charnock Richard Services**	
		3 miles	
🛏️💺✕/🔧🛒🍷	**27**	**Standish A5209**	*Page 84*
		4 miles	
🛏️💺✕/🍷	**26**	**Skelmersdale, M58, A577**	*Page 83*
		3 miles	
No Accessible Facilities	**25**	**Wigan A49**	
		3 miles	
No Accessible Facilities	**24**	**Ashton-in-Makerfield A58**	
		1 mile	
ASDA 🛏️💺✕🔧🛒🍷	**23**	**Liverpool, St Helens A580**	*Page 83*
		3 miles	
🛏️💺✕🔧 TTD 🛒🍷	**22**	**Newton-le-Willows A49**	*Page 82*
		1 mile	
No Accessible Facilities	**21a**	**M62**	
		3 miles	
🅼 🛏️💺✕/ TTD 🍷	**21**	**Warrington A57**	*Page 82*
		3 miles	
🅼 🛏️💺✕🔧	**20/20a**	**Lymm A50, M56**	*Page 81*
		5 miles	
🛏️💺✕ TTD 🍷	**19**	**Northwich, Knutsford A556**	*Page 81*
		1 mile	
	●	**Knutsford Services**	
		7 miles	
🛏️💺✕🔧🛒🍷	**18**	**Holmes Chapel, M/wich A54**	*Page 80*
		4 miles	
🛏️💺✕🔧🍷	**17**	**Congleton, Sandbach A534**	*Page 80*
		1 mile	
	●	**Sandbach Services**	
		5 miles	
🛏️💺✕/🔧🍷	**16**	**Nantwich A500**	*Page 79*
		7 miles	
	●	**Keele Services**	
		3 miles	
TWO FOR ONE 🛏️💺✕🔧 TTD 🛒🍷	**15**	**Stoke-on-Trent A500**	*Page 79*
		6 miles	
	●	**Stafford Services**	

Total Dist. **= 70 miles**

NORTH

M6 Leyland to Carlisle

NORTH

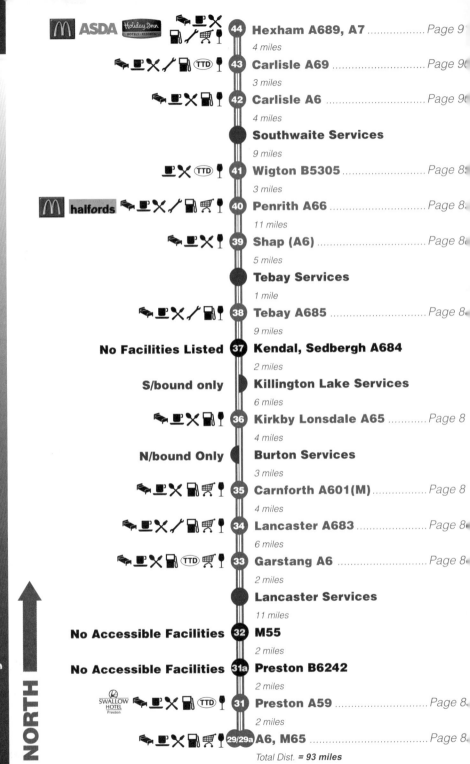

ASDA Holiday Inn	**44**	**Hexham A689, A7**	*Page 9*
		4 miles	
	43	**Carlisle A69**	*Page 90*
		3 miles	
	42	**Carlisle A6**	*Page 90*
		4 miles	
	●	**Southwaite Services**	
		9 miles	
	41	**Wigton B5305**	*Page 8*
		3 miles	
halfords	**40**	**Penrith A66**	*Page 8*
		11 miles	
	39	**Shap (A6)**	*Page 8*
		5 miles	
	●	**Tebay Services**	
		1 mile	
	38	**Tebay A685**	*Page 8*
		9 miles	
No Facilities Listed	**37**	**Kendal, Sedbergh A684**	
		2 miles	
S/bound only	▶	**Killington Lake Services**	
		6 miles	
	36	**Kirkby Lonsdale A65**	*Page 8*
		4 miles	
N/bound Only	◀	**Burton Services**	
		3 miles	
	35	**Carnforth A601(M)**	*Page 8*
		4 miles	
	34	**Lancaster A683**	*Page 8*
		6 miles	
	33	**Garstang A6**	*Page 8*
		2 miles	
	●	**Lancaster Services**	
		11 miles	
No Accessible Facilities	**32**	**M55**	
		2 miles	
No Accessible Facilities	**31a**	**Preston B6242**	
		2 miles	
SWALLOW HOTEL Preston	**31**	**Preston A59**	*Page 8*
		2 miles	
	29/29a	**A6, M65**	*Page 8*

Total Dist. = 93 miles

M6 Jn 1

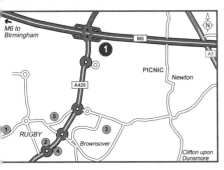

3. Spar CV21 1LT
   Tel: 01788 579491
   A426 Rugby, left at 2nd r'bout Hollowell Way

4. Tesco Supermarket and Petrol CV21 1RG
   Tel: 0845 677 9587
   A426 Rugby, on left

5. The Brownsover Hall Hotel CV21 1HU
   Tel: 01788 546100
   A426 Rugby, right at 2nd r'bout

1. Bell & Barge Restaurant CV21 1HL
   Tel: 01788 569466
   A426 Rugby, rt at r'bout into Brownsover Rd

2. Pizza Hut CV21 1SR
   Tel: 01788 550302
   A426 Rugby, right at 4th r'bout

M6 Jn 2

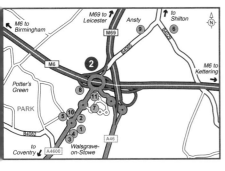

5. Campanile Hotel & Restaurant CV2 2SD
   Tel: 02476 841990
   A4600 Coventry, right at second r'bout

6. Ansty Golf Centre CV7 9JL
   Tel: 02476 621341
   B4065 Ansty, 1st right

7. Burger King CV2 2SH
   Tel: 02476 603661
   A4600 Coventry, left at r'bout

8. Hilton National Hotel CV2 2ST
   Tel: 02476 603000
   A4600 Coventry, right at r'bout

9. Rose & Castle CV7 9HZ
   Tel: 02476 612822
   B4065 Ansty, 1st roadside pub

1. **ASDA COVENTRY CV2 2PN**
   Tel: 02476 613426
   A4600 Coventry, left at 2nd r'bout

2. Holiday Inn Hotel & Restaurant CV2 2HP
   Tel: 0870 4009021
   A4600 Coventry, 100 yards on left

3. Mount Pleasant Restaurant & Pub CV2 2EU
   Tel: 02476 612406
   A4600 Coventry, on left

4. Petrol Station CV2 2EU
   Tel: 02476 602928
   A4600 Coventry

10. **MCDONALD'S RESTAURANT CV2 2RZ**
    Tel: 02476 612492
    A4600 Coventry

11. Pizza Hut CV2 2SZ
    Tel: 02476 603040
    A4600 Coventry, left at r'bout

M6 Jn 3

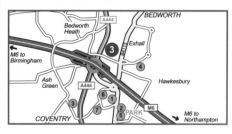

1. Longford Engine Pub & Restaurant CV6 6BP
Tel: 02476 645343
On B4113 South

2. Akash Restaurant CV6 6DR
Tel: 024 76644758
On B4113 South

3. Alexander Guest House CV6 6AY   ♿
Tel: 024 76361119
A444 Coventry, right at island, right at lights

4. Lodge Tyre Co Ltd CV7 9EJ
Tel: 024 76365246
B4113 North, right Bayton Lane

5. Nasshaa Indian Restaurant CV6 6DR
Tel: 024 76364114
On B4113 South

> **6. NOVOTEL HOTEL CV6 6HL**   ⚓ ✕ ⚒ ♟ ▤
> Tel: 02476 365000
> 98 Beds/Conf, food served daily 6am-12pm ♿
> *B4113 Bedworth, right at r'bout, on left* ♿

7. R T Windscreens CV6 6AJ
Tel: 024 76367787
B4113, Oban Rd, Woodshires Rd, left Green Lane

M6 Jn 4

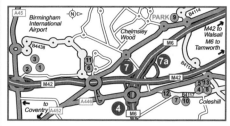

1. The Hilton Metropole Hotel B40 1PP
Tel: 0121 7804242
A446 South, over M42, in NEC Complex

2. Crowne Plaza Hotel B40 1PS
Tel: 0121 7814000
A446 South, over M42, in NEC Complex

3. Premier Lodge Hotel, Restaurant & Bar B40 1PA
Tel: 0870 9906326
A446 South, over M42, in NEC Complex

4. Coach House Hotel B46 3BG
Tel: 01675 463246
B4117 Coleshill

5. Coleshill Hotel B46 3BG
Tel: 01675 465527
B4117 Coleshill

6. Express By Holiday Inn B40 1QA
Tel: 0121 782 3222
A446 South, over M42, left at r'bout

7. George & Dragon B46 3EH
Tel: 01675 466586
B4117 Coleshill

8. Golden Tandoori B46 3BP
Tel: 01675 464945
B4117 Coleshill

9. BP Express Shopping B37 6RD
Tel: 0121 770 9828
A446 South, right A452, left at 3rd r'bout

10. Springfield House Guest House B46 3EA
Tel: 01675 465695
B4117 Coleshill South, on right

11. The Little Owl (Pub Restaurant) B40 1QA
Tel: 0121 781 0331
A446 South, over M42, left at r'bout

12. The Pepper Mill Restaurant B46 3BB
Tel: 01675 462172
B4117 Coleshill

13. Swan Hotel B46 3BL
Tel: 01675 464107
B4117 Coleshill

M6 Jn 6

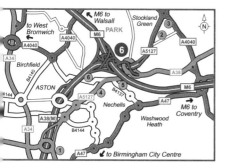

. Travel Inn & Potters Restaurant B7 4AA
Tel: 0870 2383312
A38M, 2nd exit, left at island, 1st left

. Lyndhurst Hotel B24 8QT
Tel: 0121 3735695
A5127 North, right Kingsbury Rd

3. Rollason Wood Hotel B24 8BJ
Tel: 0121 3731230
A5127 North, right A4040

4. Expressway Service Station B6 7SS
Tel: 0121 328 1186
A5127 South

5. Full House Chinese Restaurant B7 5TE
Tel: 0121 327 0919
A5127 South, left B4137

---

6. J & M TYRES LTD B6 7DE
Tel: 0121 322 2232
Tyre/valeting specialists,car,van & comm
A5127 South, 1st right, right to Electric Ave

M6 Jn 7

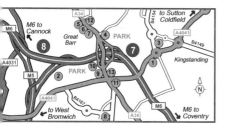

1. **ASDA** ASDA QUESLETT
B43 7HA
Tel: 0121 3600238
A34 South, left at lights, on right

. The Great Barr Hotel B43 6HS
Tel: 0121 3571141
A34 South, right at lights, signposted

. The Old Horns Public House B43 7EQ
Tel: 0121 3252930
A34 South, left at lights, at next r'bout

. Holiday Inn B43 7BG
Tel: 0870 4009009
A34 North,on right

. **BASMATI INDIAN RESTAURANT B43 7AG**
Tel: 0121 358 8898
Finest Bengali Cuisine & Balti Specialist
A34 North, on left

6. Harvester Restaurant B43 7AG
Tel: 0121 358 0242
A34 North, on left

7. Express Hotel B43 7AG
Tel: 0121 358 4044
A34 North

8. Hemstead Village Chinese Restaurant B42 1NN
Tel: 0121 358 2383
A34 South, right Old Walsall Rd

9. Raj Bangladeshi Cuisine B43 6NR
Tel: 0121 357 8368
A34 South

10. Shell Petrol Station B43 6NT
Tel: 0121 358 4622
Just South of junction

11. Somerfield Supermarket B42 1TN
Tel: 0121 357 4097
A34 South

12. Total Petrol Station B43 7AP
Tel: 0121 358 8800
A34 North

13. Tyre Sales Ltd B43 6PL
Tel: 0121 357 2378
A34 South, left A4041

M6 Jn 9

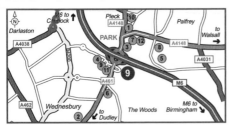

1. Abberley Hotel WS2 9AD
Tel: 01922 627413
A4148, left fork

2. BP Safeway WS10 9HA
Tel: 0121 505 2205
A461 South

3. Bescot Hotel WS2 9DG
Tel: 01922 622447
A4148 just North of junction

4. Burger King WS10 9QY
Tel: 0121 556 2100
A461 South, exit 1st slip road

5. **HALFORDS WS1 4SB**
Tel: 01922 646046
A4148 East, right Bescot Cr

6. Imperial Junction Nine Restaurant
(Cantonese and Thai) WS10 9QW
Tel: 0121 502 2218
South on A461

7. King George V WS2 9BZ
Tel: 01922 626130
A461 Walsall, right at lights, on right

8. **McDONALD'S RESTAURANT WS1 4SB**
Tel: 01922 635747
A461 North, right Wallows La, right Bescot Cr

9. Pizza Hut WS10 9QY
Tel: 0121 556 6533
A461 South, exit 1st slip rd

10. Pleck Balti WS2 9QJ
Tel: 01922 642264
A4148 North

11. KFC Restaurant WS10 9QY
A461 South, exit 1st slip road

12. Morrisons Superstore WS2 9BZ
Tel: 01922 616177
A4148 East

M6 Jn 10

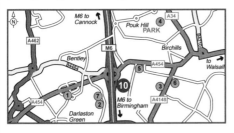

1. Brewsters & Travel Inn WS2 0WB
Tel: 0870 197 7258
A454 West

2. Cinnamon Court Indian Restaurant WS2 0BP
Tel: 0121 568 6664
B4464, left Bentley Mill Way

3. Lodge Tyre Co Ltd WS2 9EU
Tel: 01922 627772
A454 Walsall, right A4148

4. **McDONALD'S RESTAURANT WS2 1XD**
Tel: 01922 630493
A454 East, A34 North, left Stephenson Av

5. Primley Service Station WS2 8RN
Tel: 01922 634532
On A454 East

6. Tyre Stop WS2 9ES
Tel: 01922 649050
A454 Walsall, right A4148

7. Deep Pan Pizza WS2 0BP
B4464, left Bentley Mill Way

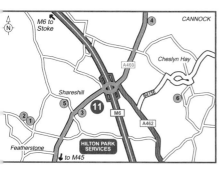

4. The Chase Gate (Pub Restaurant) WS11 1SY
   Tel: 01922 412264
   A460 East, on right

5. The Elms (Pub Restaurant) WV10 7JR
   Tel: 01922 412063
   A460 West, right Shareshill

6. The Mary Rose (Pub Restaurant) WS6 7AY
   Tel: 01922 415114
   A462, B4156, rt High St, rt Landywood Ln, rt Dundalk Ln, lt Moons Ln

. Featherstone Farm Hotel WV10 7NW &
  Tel: 01902 725371
  A460 West, right Featherstone, at crossroads

. Kings Repose Indian Cuisine WV10 7NW
  Tel: 01902 307846
  A460 West, right Featherstone, at crossroads

. Saredon Filling Station WV10 7LZ
  Tel: 01922 412995
  A460 West, on left

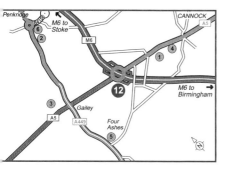

4. Tumbledown Farm (Pub Restaurant) WS11 1RU
   Tel: 01543 500891
   A5 east, on right

5. Four Ashes Inn (Pub Restaurant) WV10 7BU
   A5 west, A449 south, on left

6. Spice Mahal Restaurant ST19 5NS
   Tel: 01785 715040
   A5 west, A449 north, on right

. Oak Farm Hotel WS11 1SB
  Tel: 01543 462045
  A5 Bridgtown &

. Sommerfield Stores Ltd ST19 5NS
  Tel: 01785 715092
  A5 west, A449 north, on right

. The Spread Eagle (Pub Restaurant) ST19 5PN
  Tel: 01902 790212
  A5 west, at r'bout

M6 Jn 13

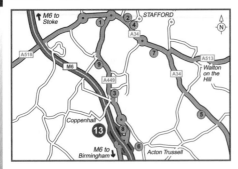

1. **Albridge Hotel ST17 4AW**
   Tel: 01785 254100
   A449 North

2. **Bailey Hotel ST17 4LL**
   Tel: 01785 214133
   A449 North, right A34

3. **Garth Hotel ST17 9JR**
   Tel: 01785 256124
   A449 North

4. **Leonard Croft Hotel ST17 4LP**
   Tel: 01785 223676
   A449 North, take A34 South, on left.

5. **S K Services Petrol Station ST17 0SU**
   Tel: 01785 662309
   A449 N, rt at r'bout, thru Acton Trussell to A34

6. **The Moat House Hotel ST17 0RJ**
   Tel: 01785 712217
   A449 North, right at r'bout

7. **The Radford Bank Inn Restaurant ST17 4PQ**
   Tel: 01785 246999
   A449 North, right A34

8. **Express By Holiday Inn ST18 9AP**
   Tel: 01785 212244
   A449 North

9. **Co-op Supermarket ST17 9LU**
   Tel: 0500 970333
   A449 North

M6 Jn 14

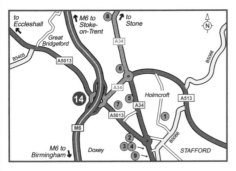

1. **ATS Euromaster Ltd ST16 3DY**
   Tel: 01785 223832
   A34, A513, right Common rd

2. **Brookhouse Petrol Station ST16 2SL**
   Tel: 01785 240010
   A5013 South

3. **KFC Restaurant ST16 2SA**
   Tel: 01785 259190
   A5013 South

4. **National Tyres And Autocare ST16 2SE**
   Tel: 01785 253641
   A5013 South

5. **North Staffs Garage - 24 hours ST16 1LD**
   Tel: 01785 255166
   On A34 South

6. **Premier Travel Inn ST16 1GZ** &
   Tel: 0870 990 6478
   A34 Stafford, on left (Business park)

7. **Tillington Hall Hotel ST16 1JJ**
   Tel: 01785 253531
   A5013 South

8. **Whitgreave Manor (Guest House) ST18 9SP**
   Tel: 01785 251767
   A34 Stoke-On-Trent, left at 2nd r'bout

9. **halfords**   **HALFORDS ST16 2DL**
   Tel: 01785 255055
   A5013 South

M6 Jn 15

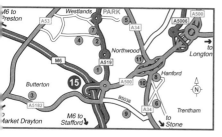

Holiday Inn ST5 4DL
Tel: 01782 557000
A519 North

Jarvis Clayton Lodge Hotel ST5 4AF
Tel: 01782 613093
A519 North

New Hayes Farm Bed & Breakfast ST5 4DX
Tel: 01782 680889
At r'bout take Shrewsbury exit (A5182), follow A53.

Rose Of Kashmir ST5 4AN
Tel: 01782 610508
A519 North, left Seabridge La, 3rd left Orwell Pl

5. Tesco Supermarket ST4 6PL
Tel: 0845 677 9660
A500, A34 North

6.
| TWO FOR ONE |
ALL DAY • EVERY DAY

**THE BULLS HEAD
ST4 8EN**
Tel: 01782 642318
2-4-1 all day everyday-large function room
A500 Stoke, A34 South, 2nd left, on right

7. The Gatehouse Public House ST5 3HR
Tel: 01782 615332
A519 North, on left

8. Total Petrol Station ST4 4QA
Tel: 01782 654800
A500, right A34

9. Trentham Park Golf Club ST4 8AE
Tel: 01782 658800
Right at junction r'bout, left Whitmore Road

10. Trentside Private Hotel ST4 8NJ
Tel: 01782 642443
A500, right at r'bout, on right

11. White House Hotel ST4 6SP
Tel: 01782 642460
A500, at r'bout

M6 Jn 16

Azzurri Italian Restaurant ST7 2HA
Tel: 01270 883555
On B5077 East

Barthomley Service Area CW2 5PS
Tel: 01270 883212
West of junction

Holly Trees Hotel ST7 2JL
Tel: 01270 876847
B5078 Radway Green, right at T-junction

Kashmir Garden Restaurant ST7 2HA
Tel: 01270 884475
On B5077 East

Little Chef CW2 5PT
Tel: 01270 883115
West of junction

6. Manor House Hotel ST7 2QQ
Tel: 01270 884000
A500 Stoke, take first exit Audley/Alsager

7. The Chinese Garden Restaurant ST7 2JA
Tel: 01270 877081
On B5077 East

8. The Lodge Tyre ST7 2LX
Tel: 01270 873052
B5077 East, rt at Sandbach Rd, lt at Fields Rd

9. The Plough Inn ST7 2JN
Tel: 01270 882085
On B5077 East

10. The White Lion Inn CW2 5PG
Tel: 01270 882242
3rd exit Alsager/Barthomley, 1st left Barthomley

11. Travel Lodge CW2 5PT
Tel: 01270 883157
West of Junction

12. Poacher's Pocket Restaurant ST7 2UB
On B5077 East

M6 Jn 17

3. SAXON CROSS HOTEL & RESTAURANT
Tel: 01270 763281   **CW11 1SE**
52 e/s rooms, fresh food & extensive menu
A534 Congleton, immediate left, on left

4. LA CAMMINATA CW11 1AR
Tel: 0870 2244140
Best pizza outside Italy (secret recipe)!
A534 Sandbach, 3rd exit at r'about, rt at s'market

5. CAFÉ SYMPHONY SANDBACH RESTAURANT &
Tel: 01270 763664   **WINE BAR CW11 1HG**
Bar, restaurant, light meals, coffees
A534 Sandbach, right to town centre, on right

1.   THE BEAR'S HEAD CW11 1RS
Tel: 01477 544732
Great value food all day every day.
A534 Congleton, lt to A5022, lt to A50, on right

6. Petrol Station CW11 4SP
Tel: 01270 758980
A534 Sandbach, right to town centre

7. Chimney House Hotel CW11 4ST
Tel: 01270 764141
A534 Congleton

8. China Kitchen Chinese Restaurant CW11 1AH
Tel: 01270 762777
A534 South, right High Street

2.   THE OLD HALL HOTEL CW11 1AL
Tel: 01270 761221
Beautiful four hundred year old Tudor hotel
A534 Sandbach, right at lights, on left

M6 Jn 18

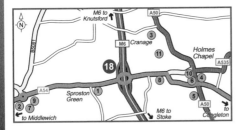

5. Fortune City Chinese Restaurant CW4 7BD
Tel: 01477 532861
A54 East, right London Rd (A50)

6. Holly Lodge Hotel CW4 7AS
Tel: 01477 537033
A54 H/Chapel, rt A54 Congleton, lt at lights (A50)

7. Little Chef CW10 0JB
Tel: 01606 834700
A54 West

8. Texaco Petrol Station CW4 7ES
Tel: 01477 532056
A54 East

9. Travelodge CW10 0JB
Tel: 01606 738229
A54 West

10. Co-Op Supermarket CW4 7AJ
Tel: 01477 532113
A54 East, left London Rd (A50)

11. Ye Olde Vicarage Hotel CW4 8EF
Tel: 01477 532041
A54 East, A50 North

1.   THE FOX & HOUNDS INN CW4 7LW
Tel: 01606 832303
Family run, good home cooking & real ale
A54 Middlewich, 400 yards on left

2. Burger King CW10 0JB
A54 West

3. Cranage Hall Hotel CW4 8EW
Tel: 01477 536666
A54 East, A50 North

4. Balti Massala Indian Restaurant CW4 7AP
Tel: 01477 535880
A54 East, left London Rd (A50)

M6 Jn 19

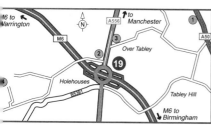

Cottons Hotel WA16 0SU
Tel: 01565 650333
A556 North, right through to A50, left

2. Little Chef WA16 0PP
Tel: 01565 755049
A556 North

3. Old Vicarage Guest House WA16 0PL
Tel: 01565 652221
A556 North, right Over Tabley

4. Heyrose Golf Club WA16 0HZ &
Tel: 01526 733664
Follow tourist signs on s/side of r'bout, on rt.

M6 Jn 20

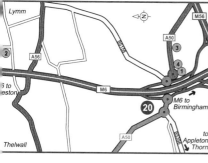

Travelodge WA13 0SP
Tel: 0870 191 1657
A50 East, at services

2. Statham Lodge Hotel WA13 9BP
Tel: 01925 752204
B5158, left A56, 2nd right, left, on right

3. Total Petrol WA13 0TE
Tel: 01925 750810
A50 East, on right

4. **MCDONALD'S RESTAURANT
WA13 0SP**
Tel: 01925 758759
A50 East, on r'bout

M6 Jn 21

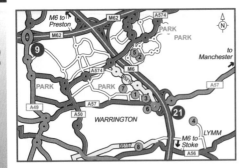

1. ATS Euromaster Ltd WA1 4RT
Tel: 01925 815612
A57, take B5210, left Hardwick, left

2. Burger King WA3 7PQ
Tel: 01925 812426
B5210, rt over M6, rt Oakwood Ct, rt Dewhurst Rd, on lt

3. Holiday Inn (Warrington) WA1 4PX
Tel: 0870 400 9087
A57 West, at junction

4. Lymm Golf Club WA13 9AN
Tel: 01925 752177
A57 West, A50 South, A56 east, left through Lymm

5. **MCDONALD'S RESTAURANT** ♨ ⎙
WA3 7PQ ✕ ☕
Tel: 01925 850729
B5210, rt over M6, rt Oakwood Ct, rt Dewhurst Rd, on

6. Premier Lodge WA1 4GB
Tel: 0870 990 6524
A57 West, at junction

7. Sindh Indian Cuisine WA1 4EP
Tel: 01925 823396
2nd right on A57 West ♿

8. The Little Manor Restaurant WA4 2SX
Tel: 01925 261703
A57 West, A50 South, left B5157

M6 Jn 22

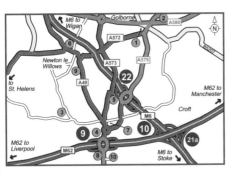

1. **INNKEEPERS LODGE & TOBY CARVERY RESTAURANT WA3 1HD**
Tel: 01942 671421
More than a good nights sleep
A579 North, right T-Junction, on left ♿

2. Texaco Star Lane Head WA3 2BD ♿
Tel: 01942 208073
A579 North, rt at T-Junc, on rt after lights

3. Alder Root Golf Club WA2 8RZ
Tel: 01925 291919
Left to island, right at lights, left, 1st right

4. Burger King WA2 8RD
Tel: 01925 573387
South to M62 J9

5. Hermit Inn WA2 8SN
Tel: 01925 224042
South from junction, A573 North

6. Pied Bull Hotel WA12 9SH
Tel: 01925 224549
A49 North

7. The Swan Tavern & Premier Lodge WA2 8LF
Tel: 01925 631416
South from junction, bear right

8. Brewers Fayre & Travel Inn WA2 8RN
Tel: 01925 414417
South to M62 J9, on right

9. Total Petrol Station WA12 8BS
Tel: 01925 290864
A49 North

10. Co-op Supermarket WA2 9SF
Tel: 01925 445789
A49 South, left Sandy Lane, left Cotswold Rd

M6 Jn 23

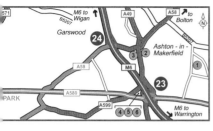

3. Angel Hotel WN4 9PL
Tel: 01942 728704
A49 North, on left ♿

4. Holiday Inn WA12 0JG
Tel: 0870 400 9039
A580 West, at junction

5. Shell Petrol Station WA12 0HL
Tel: 01925 293690
A580 West, at junction

6. Thistle Haydock Hotel WA11 9SG
Tel: 01942 272000
A580 West, at junction

ASDA GOLBORNE WA3 3SP
Tel: 01942 723231
A580 East, left Park Rd, Barn Lane, Bank St ⛽ £ 🛒 ♿

Premier Travel Inn & Millers Kitchen WN4 9PT
Tel: 0870 9906582
A49 to Wigan, beside Haydock Park

M6 Jn 26

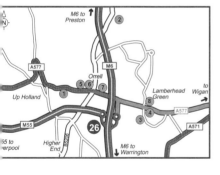

4. Pemberton Tyres WN5 8JR
Tel: 01942 222413
A577 East, right Chapel St

5. Stag Inn WN5 8QU
Tel: 01942 211067
On A577 West

6. Trattoria Pizzeria Sorrento WN5 8QJ
Tel: 01942 218555
Left at lights, next right ♿

7. Travel Inn & Beefeater Restaurant WN5 8HQ
Tel: 0870 197 7271
On A577 West

8. KFC Restaurant WN5 8HE
Tel: 01942 216849
On A577 East

Abbey Lakes Inn & Lodge WN5 8QZ
Tel: 01695 622664
A577 West, on left ♿

Vale Royal Brewers Fayre WN5 0LH ♿
Tel: 01942 223700
A577 West, rt at post office, under m/way, 1st rt

A G Tyres WN5 8JS
Tel: 01942 226007
A577 East, right Chapel St

M6 Jn 27

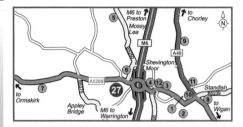

1. THE BEECHES HOTEL & BRASSERIE WN6 0TD
Tel: 01257 426432
Privately owned brasserie - open all day
A5209 East, left at T-junction, on left

2. THE DOG & PARTRIDGE PUBLIC HOUSE WN6 0TG
Tel: 01257 401218
Real ale a speciality, outside heated area
A5209 East, left at T-junction, on right

3. Premier Travel Inn & Charnley Arms WN6 0SS
Tel: 0870 9906474
A5209 East, left

4. T.C.S. Standish (Total Petrol) WN6 0SR
Tel: 01257 473660
A5209 East, lt at T-junc, lt Almond Brook Rd

5. La Primera Taverna (Tapas Restaurant) WN6 9RN
Tel: 01257 421168
B5250 North

6. BP Express Shopping Ltd WN6 9RB
Tel: 01257 421390
A5209 West, on right

7. The Wiggin Tree Pub & Restaurant WN8 7TG
Tel: 01257 462318
A5209 West, on left

8. ATS Euromaster Ltd WN6 0HW
Tel: 01257 423146
A5209 East, over cross roads

9. Cinnamon Indian Cuisine WN6 0QD
Tel: 01257 426661
A49 North, Preston Rd.

10. Somerfield Supermarket WN6 0TD
Tel: 01257 427080
A5209 East

11. Standish Service Station WN6 0JF
Tel: 01257 422899
A5209 East to Standish centre, left A49, on right

12. Wigan Standish Moat House WN6 0SR
Tel: 01257 499988
A5209 East, on left

M6 Jn 28

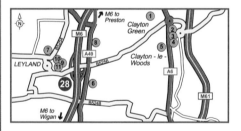

1. **ASDA** ASDA CLAYTON GREEN
PR6 7JY
Tel: 01772 335779
B5256 East, on left

2. The Pines Hotel PR6 7ED
Tel: 01772 338551
B5256 East, right at r'about to A6, on left

3. The Halfway House Pub & Restaurant PR6 7JB
Tel: 01772 334477
B5256 East, right at r'about, on left

4. Travelodge Preston Chorley PR6 7JB
Tel: 0870 1911671
B5256 East, right at r'about, on left

5. Shell Garage PR6 7JD
Tel: 01772 695870
B5256 East, right to A6, on right

6. Leyland Golf Club PR25 5UD
Tel: 01772 436457
A49 South

7. MCDONALD'S RESTAURANT
PR25 3LZ
Tel: 01772 623643
B5256 West, 2nd exit at r'about

8. Rydal Petroleum PR25 5UE
Tel: 01772 455253
A49 North

9. The Beijing Restaurant PR25 3NH
Tel: 01772 459122
B5256 West, right at r'about

10. The Viceroy (Indian Restaurant) PR25 3NP
Tel: 01772 621031
B5256 West, right at r'bout, left Golden Hill Lane

11. Casa-Caterina PR25 3NH
Tel: 01772 423344
B5256 West, right at r'bout

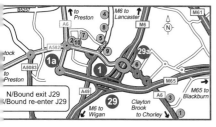

5. Farmhouse Kitchen PR5 6EJ
Tel: 01772 334334
B6258 Bamberbridge, on left after lights

6. Novotel PR5 8AA
Tel: 01772 313331
At junction

7. Sainsburys Supermarket PR5 6BJ
Tel: 01772 627762
A6 West, right Station Rd, left Mavelock Rd

8. Titash Tandoori PR5 6EH
Tel: 01772 337744
B6258 North

9. Ye Olde Hob Inn PR5 6EP
Tel: 01772 336863
B6258 North

10. Premier Lodge & Millers Restaurant PR5 6BA
Tel: 01772 324100
A6 West

Brook House Hotel PR6 7EH
Tel: 01772 336403
A6 Chorley, through three r'bout's, on left

Burger King PR5 6BA
Tel: 01772 337192
West of junction

Clayton Brook Service Station PR6 7EJ
Tel: 01772 336064
A6 South

Dario's Take-Away PR5 6EA
Tel: 01772 697070
B6258 Bamberbridge, on left

M6 Jn 31

4. Huntley's of Samlesbury (Farm Shop & Tea Room) PR5 0UN
Tel: 01772 877123
A59 Clitheroe, left onto Whalley Road, on left ♿

5. Premier Lodge & Millers Kitchen BB2 7LE
Tel: 0870 9906388
A59 Clitheroe, left onto Whalley Road, on left

6. Quattros Italian Restaurant PR5 0UP
Tel: 01772 877800
A59 Clitheroe, A677

7. Fishwick Hall Golf Club PR1 5TD
Tel: 01772 798300
A59 West, 1st left, on left

8. New Hall Tavern PR5 0XA
Tel: 01772 877217
A59 Clitheroe, first right, right to B6230

9. BP Tickled Trout Services PR5 0UJ
Tel: 01772 877656
A59 Preston New Road ♿

THE SWALLOW HOTEL - 3 STAR
SWALLOW HOTEL Preston
Tel: 01772 87735178   **PR5 0UL**
78 En-suite bedrooms.
Leisure facilities.
A59 East, on left at junction of A59/A677

MacDonald Tickled Trout Hotel PR5 0UJ
Tel: 01772 877671
Situated at junction, next to BP Garage ♿

BP New Hall Lane Filling Station PR1 4TE
Tel: 01772 794212
A59 West, on left

M6 Junctions **29a & 31**

85

M6 Jn 33

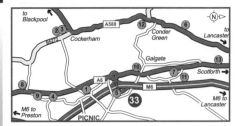

1. **The Bay Horse Inn** LA2 0HR
   01524 791204
   A6 Preston, 2nd left, on right &

2. **Asian Spice Indian Restaurant** LA2 0EF
   015242 63400
   A6 South, right Cockerham, right

3. **Bumbles Restaurant** LA2 0EF
   01524 791264
   A6 South, right Cockerham, right

4. **El Nido Spanish Restaurant** PR3 0AE
   01524 791254
   A6 Preston, on left

5. **Hampson House Hotel** LA2 0JB
   01524 751158
   A6 South, left Hampson Lane

6. **Lancaster Golf Club** LA2 0AJ
   01524 751247
   In Galgate turn left Condor Green, right on A588

7. **Lancaster House Hotel** LA1 4GJ   &
   01524 844822
   A6 North Lancaster, on right on Green Lane.

8. **Middle Holly Cottage Guest House** PR3 1AH
   01524 792399
   A6 South, off on right

9. **New Holly Hotel** PR3 0BL
   01524 791424
   A6 South

10. **Plough Inn** LA2 0LQ   &
    01524 751337
    Right at r'bout, half mile on left

11. **Spar** LA1 4XX
    01524 65775
    A6 North, right Green Lane, left

12. **Thurnham Mill Hotel & Brasserie** LA2 0BD
    01524 752852
    A6 North, lt in Galgate, signs Condor Green, lt

13. **Toll Bar Lancaster Petrol Station** LA1 4NP
    Tel: 01524 63394
    A6 North

M6 Jn 34

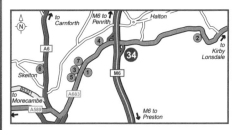

1. Brewsters & Travel Inn LA1 3PE
   Tel: 01524 384800
   A683 West, on left   &

2. The Scarthwaite Country House Hotel LA2 9HR
   Tel: 01524 770267
   A683 Kirkby Lonsdale, on right   &

3. Shell Garage LA1 3PE
   Tel: 01524 590900
   A683 West

4. Holiday Inn LA1 3RA
   Tel: 0870 400 9047
   A683 West of junction

5. Lancaster Town House (Guest House) LA1 3PB
   Tel: 01524 65527
   A683 West

6. Spar LA1 2HL
   Tel: 01524 63050
   A683 West, right A589, A6

7. National Tyres And Autocare LA1 3PE
   Tel: 01524 69568
   A683 West, right Lansil Way

16 Jn 35

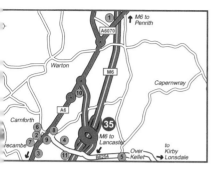

Longlands Hotel & Restaurant LA6 1JH
Tel: 01524 781256
A6 North, A6070

Carnforth Hotel LA5 9LD
Tel: 01524 732902
On A6 South

Carnforth Service Station LA5 9EA
Tel: 01524 733547
On A6 South

Cross Keys Hotel LA5 9LR
Tel: 01524 732749
On B6254

5. Eagles Head Hotel LA6 1DL
Tel: 01524 732457
B6524 Over Kellet, right at Green

6. Royal Station Hotel LA5 9BT
Tel: 01524 732033
Off A6 on Market St

7. Safeway Supermarket LA5 9LE
Tel: 01524 737720
On A6 South

8. The Blue Mango Café LA5 9JY
Tel: 01524 735093
Signs to Carnforth, on left as you approach traffic lights.

9. The County Hotel LA5 9LD
Tel: 01524 732469
On A6

---

10. TRUCK HAVEN LORRY PARK & FILLING STATION
Tel: 01524 736699   **LA5 9RQ** HGV
Home cooked food, 25 e/s beds, cctv/secty
A6 Carnforth, left at 2 r'bouts

---

11. Ikys II Indian Restaurant LA5 9AJ
Tel: 01524 733500
Off B6254 on Highfield Rd

16 Jn 36

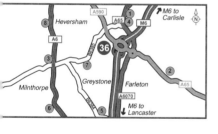

CROOKLANDS HOTEL LA7 7NW
Tel: 01539 567432
Quality that discerning travellers expect
A65 North, on right

The Plough Hotel LA6 1PJ
Tel: 015395 67227
On A65 South

Cross Keys Hotel LA7 7AB
Tel: 015395 62115
A65 North, left B6385, at cross roads

4. M6 Diesel Services LA7 7NX
Tel: 015395 67280
On A65 North

5. Smithy Inn LA6 1PS
Tel: 01524 781302
A6070, follow Holme signposts

6. The Wheatsheaf Hotel LA7 7AL
Tel: 015395 62123
A65 North, left B6385, left A6, on right

7. Station Hotel LA7 7LR
Tel: 015395 62345
A65 North, left B6385

8. The Blue Bell Hotel LA7 7FH
Tel: 015395 62018
A65 North, left B6385, right A6

M6 Jn 38

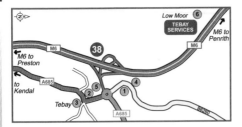

1. Tebay Vehicle Repairs CA10 3SS
   Tel: 01539 624341
   Left at r'bout on right

2. **CROSS KEYS INN CA10 3UY** &
   Tel: 01539 624240
   500 yr old little gem, excellent food, B & B
   A685 Kendal, on right

3. **HIGH BANK HOUSE (GUEST HOUSE) CA10 3T**
   Tel: 01539 624651
   2 single room/2 double room/1 twin room
   Right at r'bout, left in village centre

4. M6 Diesel Services CA10 3SS
   Tel: 01539 624336
   1st left at r'bout, B6260, on left &

5. Primrose Cottage (Guest House) CA10 3TL
   Tel: 01539 624791
   Right at r'bout, on right &

6. Westmorland Hotel CA10 3SB
   Tel: 01539 624351
   Via Tebay Services

M6 Jn 39

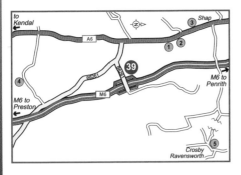

1. Brookfield Guest House CA10 3PZ
   Tel: 01931 716397
   A6 North

2. Greyhound Hotel CA10 3PW
   Tel: 01931 716474
   A6 Shap, on right &

3. Kings Arms Hotel CA10 3NU &
   Tel: 01931 716277
   A6 Shap, on left at entrance to village

4. Shap Wells Hotel CA10 3QU
   Tel: 01931 716628
   A6 South, left turn

5. The Butchers Arms CA10 3JP
   Tel: 01931 715202
   A6 North, right Crosby Ravensworth

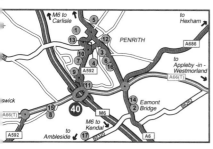

ATS Euromaster CA11 9BL
Tel: 01768 865656
A592 North, left, left Norfolk Rd, rt Gilwilly Rd

Beehive Inn CA10 2BX
Tel: 01768 862081
A66 East, right at r'bout &

Bewick Coffee House CA11 7BJ
Tel: 01768 864764
Penrith Centre, Princes Street car park &

Board & Elbow CA11 7DA
Tel: 01768 867221
Follow signs to Town Centre, bear left

Brooklands Guest House CA11 7QN
Tel: 01768 863395
One way system, left at Town Hall

Caledonia Guest House CA11 8HR
Tel: 01768 864482
A66 East, left at r'bout, on left

---

halfords **HALFORDS**
CA11 7JQ
Tel: 01768 892960
At r'bout take A592 Penrith

---

8. Little Chef CA11 0DT
   Tel: 01768 868303
   A66 West, on left

9. Mark Johnss Petrol CA11 7EH
   Tel: 01768 892906
   Take A529 Penrith

---

10. **MCDONALD'S RESTAURANT**
    CA11 7JQ
    Tel: 01768 868347
    A592 Penrith, on left next to train station

---

11. North Lakes Hotel CA11 8QT
    Tel: 01768 868111
    On A592 Penrith

12. Purple Sage Restaurant CA11 7YE
    Tel: 01768 895555
    Head for Penrith Town Ctr, behind Barclays bank

13. Safeway Supermarket CA11 7JN
    Tel: 01768 867631
    A592 Penrith, bear left

14. The Crown CA10 2BX
    Tel: 01768 892092
    A6 South, on left &

15. Travelodge CA11 0DT
    Tel: 01768 866958
    A66 West, on left

16. Tynedale Guest House CA11 8HR
    Tel: 01768 867491
    A66 East, A6 Penrith

17. Yanwath Gate Inn CA10 2LF
    Tel: 01768 862386
    A66 East, right at 2 r'bouts, on right

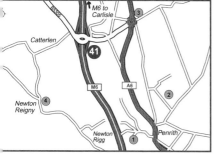

Doug's Diner CA11 9BN
Tel: 01768 892310
A6 S, rt B'swick Rd, rt N'folk Rd, Gilwilly Ind. Est

2. Penrith Golf Club CA11 8SG
   Tel: 01768 891919
   A6 South, left Salkeld Rd

3. Stoneybeck Inn CA11 8RP
   Tel: 01768 862369
   B5305, at r'bout

4. Sun Inn CA11 0AP &
   Tel: 01768 867055
   B5305 N, lt Catterlen, lt at T-junc for N.Reigny

M6 Jn 42

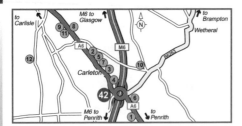

1. COUNTRY HOUSE B&B CA4 0BT
Tel: 016974 73381
Homely service, TV, lovely views, quiet
A6 Penrith, on right

2. Terracotta Restaurant CA1 3DP
Tel: 01228 524433
A6 Carlisle, on right &

3. BP Petrol Station CA4 0AA
Tel: 01228 592479
A6 North

4. Brewers Fayre & Travel Inn CA4 0AD
Tel: 01228 532073
A6 North, at junction

5. Dhaka Tandoori CA1 3DS
Tel: 01228 523855
A6 North

6. Golden Fleece Service Station CA4 0AN
Tel: 01228 542766
A6 Penrith, at r'bout

7. Greenbank Inn CA1 3DP
Tel: 01228 528846
A6 North

8. Harraby Inn CA1 2QN
Tel: 01228 524647
A6 Carlisle, on right

9. Kenilworth Guest House CA1 2PZ
Tel: 01228 526179
A6 Carlisle, on left &

10. Lowther Arms CA4 8DL
Tel: 01228 560905
B6263, 1st left

11. Pinegrove Hotel CA1 2QS
Tel: 01228 524828
A6 Carlisle, on left &

12. The White Ox Inn CA2 4SQ
Tel: 01228 532754
Dalston exit, right to Durdar Rd, on left

M6 Jn 43

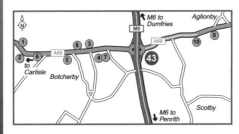

1. WHITELEA GUEST HOUSE CA1 1LP
Tel: 01228 533139
En-suite bedrooms, non-smoking
A69 to Carlisle, after 3 lights, on right

2. CHERRYGROVE B&B CA1 2AW
Tel: 01228 541942
Nice rooms, good food, disc. 3 or more nights
A69 to Carlisle, after 4 lights, on left

3. Tesco Supermarket CA1 2SB
Tel: 0845 6779125
A69 Carlisle, on right

4. Shepherds Inn & Auctioneer CA1 2RW
Tel: 01228 539766
A69 Carlisle, left at lights, on left &

5. Travel Inn & Brewsters CA1 2WF
Tel: 08701 977053
A69 Carlisle, half mile on left &

6. The Beehive Pub CA1 1LH
Tel: 01228 549731
A69 to Carlisle, after 3 lights, on left

7. ATS Euromaster Ltd CA1 2RW
Tel: 01228 525277
A69 West, left Montgomery Way

8. Brunton Park Service Station CA1 2RZ
Tel: 01228 528715
On A69 West

9. Carlisle Golf Club CA4 8AG
Tel: 01228 513029
A69 Newcastle, signposted on right

10. Waterloo Inn CA4 8AG
Tel: 01228 513347
A69 East &

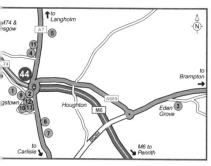

5. Dandy Dinmont Camping & Caravan Park CA6 4EA
Tel: 01228 674611
A7 North, on right &

6. Newfield Grange Hotel CA3 0AF
Tel: 01228 819926
A7 Carlisle, turn left when signed, on right

7. Premier Lodge & Millers Kitchen CA3 0AT
Tel: 0870 9906502
A7 Carlisle, on left &

8. Gallo Rosso Restaurant CA6 4BY
Tel: 01228 526037
A7 Carlisle, 1st right, on left

9. Night Owl Truckstop Motel CA3 0JR
Tel: 01228 534192
A7 Carlisle, right at lights, on right

10. Gates Tyres Super Centre CA3 0EX
Tel: 01228 529656
A7 South, right at 2nd lights, right Parkhill Rd

11. Harker Service Station CA6 4DT
Tel: 01228 674274
A7 North

**ASDA CARLISLE
CA3 0JQ**
Tel: 01228 526550
A7 Carlisle, 1st right, on left

**THE HOLIDAY INN
CA3 0HR**
Tel: 0870 4009018
Relax and be yourself
A7 Carlisle, right at lights, next right

THE STAGG INN PUB & RESTAURANT CA6 4QN
Tel: 01228 573210
Excellent food in a cosy pub
A689 Hexham, left at r'bout, 2nd right

Border Garden Centre & Café CA6 4DS
Tel: 01228 674676
A7 North, 1st on left &

---

12. **MCDONALD'S RESTAURANT
CA3 0ET**
Tel: 01228 513309
A7 South, right at lights &

---

13. Partco Autoparts Ltd CA3 0HA
Tel: 01228 524161
A7 South, right at 2nd lights

THINK
Make Time For A Break
www.thinkroadsafety.gov.uk

M74/A74(M) Summary

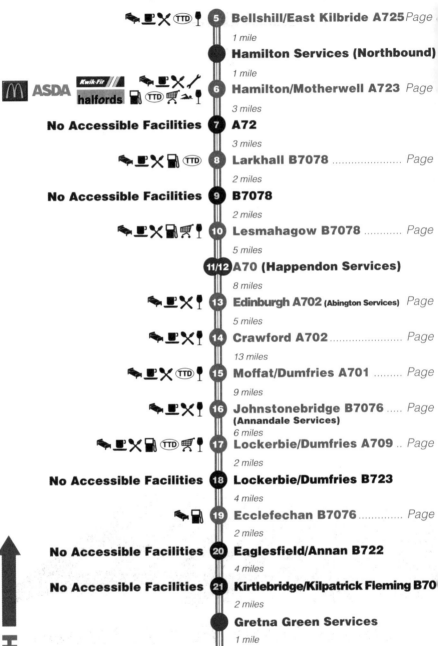

🛏️🅿️✗⑪🍷 **5** **Bellshill/East Kilbride A725** *Page*

1 mile

⚫ **Hamilton Services (Northbound)**

1 mile

🅼 ASDA *Kwik-Fit* halfords 🛏️🅿️✗🔧 ⛽⑪🍴🔧🍷 **6** **Hamilton/Motherwell A723** *Page*

3 miles

No Accessible Facilities **7** **A72**

3 miles

🛏️🅿️✗⛽⑪ **8** **Larkhall B7078** .... *Page*

2 miles

No Accessible Facilities **9** **B7078**

2 miles

🛏️🅿️✗⛽🛒🍷 **10** **Lesmahagow B7078** .... *Page*

5 miles

11/12 **A70 (Happendon Services)**

8 miles

🛏️🅿️✗🍷 **13** **Edinburgh A702** (Abington Services) *Page*

5 miles

🛏️🅿️✗🍷 **14** **Crawford A702** .... *Page*

13 miles

🛏️🅿️✗⑪🍷 **15** **Moffat/Dumfries A701** .... *Page*

9 miles

🛏️🅿️✗🍷 **16** **Johnstonebridge B7076** ..... *Page*
(Annandale Services)

6 miles

🛏️🅿️✗⛽⑪🛒🍷 **17** **Lockerbie/Dumfries A709** .. *Page*

2 miles

No Accessible Facilities **18** **Lockerbie/Dumfries B723**

4 miles

🛏️⛽ **19** **Ecclefechan B7076** .... *Page*

2 miles

No Accessible Facilities **20** **Eaglesfield/Annan B722**

4 miles

No Accessible Facilities **21** **Kirtlebridge/Kilpatrick Fleming B70**

2 miles

⚫ **Gretna Green Services**

1 mile

No Accessible Facilities **22** **Longtown/Gretna Green**

1 mile

No Accessible Facilities **23** **Annan A75**

Total Dist. **= 74 miles**

No Accessible Facilities 1️⃣ **Tollcross A74**

0.5 miles

No Accessible Facilities 2️⃣ **A765**

2.5 miles

No Accessible Facilities 3️⃣ **A721**

0.5 miles

🛏️💷✕🍷 4️⃣ **M73; Uddingston A74** .... *Page 94*

2 miles

Bothwell Services (Southbound)

1 mile

🛏️💷✕ⓉⓉⒹ🍷 5️⃣ **Bellshill/East Kilbride A725** *Page 94*

Total Dist. **= 6.5 miles**

M74 Jn 4

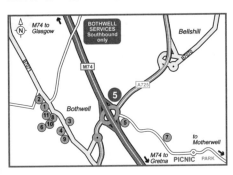

1. Mail Coach Restaurant G71 7SG
Tel: 0141 771 1569
A74 West, on right

2. Travel Inn & Blackbear Beefeater G71 7SA
Tel: 0870 197 7109
A74, next to Zoo Park (now closed)

3. White Pillars Guest House G71 7SG
Tel: 0141 773 1170
A74 West, on right

M74 Jn 5

1. Amran Tandoori G71 8ER
Tel: 01698 852330
A725 Bothwell, right at r'bout, on Main St

2. Bothwell Bridge Hotel G71 8EU
Tel: 01698 852246
A725 Bothwell, on left

3. China Cottage Restaurant G71 8NB
Tel: 01698 852217
A725 Bothwell, on right

4. Da Luciano Italian Restaurant G71 8SE
Tel: 01698 852722
A725 Bothwell, on left

5. Holiday Inn Express ML1 3RB
Tel: 01698 858585
At junction, West of motorway

6. Lisini Court (Guest House) G71 8DG
Tel: 01698 853482
A725 Bothwell, left Mill Road, left Fife Cr

7. M & D Theme Park ML1 3RT
Tel: 01698 333777
Take Strathclyde Park exit at junction

8. Riva Italian Restaurant G71 8RD
Tel: 01698 850888
A725 Bothwell, on main street

9. The Cricklewood Hotel G71 8LZ
Tel: 01698 853172
A725 Bothwell, on left

10. The Grape Vine Restaurant G71 8RD
Tel: 01698 852014
A725 Bothwell, on main street

11. Winnifred's Restaurant G71 8RD
Tel: 01698 854526
A725 Bothwell, on main street

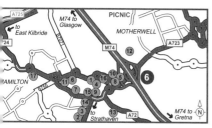

8. MCDONALD'S RESTAURANT ML3 6AD
Tel: 01698 207990
West to Hamilton, rt r'bout, rt next r'bout

Bombay Cottage (Restaurant) ML3 6HW
Tel: 01698 286957
A723, right at r'bout, left Auchingramont Rd

Butterburn Bar ML3 7JQ
Tel: 01698 283357
A723 Hamilton, follow Strathaven to Town Centre

Di Maggios Italian Restaurant ML3 7JQ
Tel: 01698 891828
A723 Hamilton, follow Strathaven

Don Jose Restaurant ML3 7BQ
Tel: 01698 284023
A723, left at r'bout, on Townhead St

halfords HALFORDS ML3 6AD
Tel: 01698 283323
A723, right at r'bout

Hamilton Water Palace (Pool) ML3 0HQ
Tel: 01698 459950
A723, right A72, left at r'bout, Almada St

Kwik-Fit KWIK-FIT ML3 6PA
Tel: 01698 200373
A723, left at r'bout, rt Patrick St

9. Pietruccio Italian Restaurant ML3 6AS
Tel: 01698 540665
A723, rt Cadzow St, left Campbell St

10. Pizza Hut ML3 6AD
Tel: 01698 200000
A723, right at r'bout

11. Royal Blossom Restaurant ML3 0HQ
Tel: 01698 282811
A723, right A72, left Almada St

12. Strathclyde Country Park ML1 3ED
Tel: 01698 266155
A723 Motherwell, on left

13. The Avonbridge ML3 7DB
Tel: 01698 420525
A723, bear left Townhead St

14. Yee Hong Restaurant ML3 6QL
Tel: 01698 283445
A723, follow Strathaven, right Kemp St

15. Somerfield Supermarket ML3 6AH
Tel: 01698 429231
A723, at r'bout take Keith St, then Quarry St

16. ASDA ASDA HAMILTON ML3 6AD
Tel: 01698 456700
A723, right at r'bout

17. Petrol Station ML3 9AN
Tel: 01698 286636
A723, right A72, left Almada St, rt Burnbank Rd

174 Jn 8

Carlin Cottage Guest House ML9 1HU
Tel: 01698 884084
On B7078 North

2. Larkhall Golf Course ML9 3AB
Tel: 01698 881113
A71 North, left B7019

3. Shawlands Hotel ML9 2TZ
Tel: 01698 791111
On A71 North

4. Shell Petrol Station ML9 1HX
Tel: 01698 880110
On B7078 North

5. The Coffee Pot ML9 3EF
Tel: 01698 792799
A71 Stonehouse, left at r'bout

M74 Jn 10

S.bound exit at J9

Kirkmuirhill

to Strathaven

Lesmahagow

M74 to Glasgow

M74 to Gretna

1. **Bent Brae Bistro ML11 9RP**
   Tel: 01555 895753
   B7078 North, left Strathaven

2. **Costcutter Supermarket ML11 0AA**
   Tel: 01555 893329
   B7078 South

3. **Fourways Service Station Ltd ML11 9RN**
   Tel: 01555 893498
   B7078 North, left Strathaven

4. **I Mcinally Guest House ML11 0JQ**
   Tel: 01555 892226
   B7078 North, left Strathaven

5. **Masons Arms Hotel ML11 0EQ**
   Tel: 01555 893944
   B7078 South, off to right

6. **Riverside Service Station ML11 0DU**
   Tel: 01555 895157
   B7078 South, off to right

7. **Co-op Supermarket ML11 0EQ**
   Tel: 01555 894008
   B7078 South, off to right

8. **Southfield Hotel ML11 9RZ**
   Tel: 01555 892233
   B7078 North

9. **The Poachers Restaurant ML11 9RW**
   Tel: 01555 895237
   B7078 North, left Strathaven

M74 Jn 13

M74 to Glasgow

to Edinburgh

Nether Abington

to Carlisle

Abington

1. **Abington Hotel ML12 6SD**
   Tel: 01864 502467
   Follow signs to Abington Village, less than a mile

2. **Days Inn ML12 6RG**
   Tel: 01864 502782
   A702 North, on left

M74 Jn 14

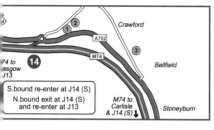

1. Heatherghyll Motel ML12 6TW   ♿
   Tel: 01864 502641
   At bottom of slip road off motorway (S/bound)

2. Holmlands ML12 6TW
   Tel: 01864 502753
   On A702

3. The Crawford Arms Hotel ML12 6TP
   Tel: 01864 502267
   Off A702 in Crawford

M74 Jn 15

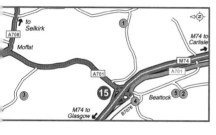

Barnhill Springs DG10 9QS
Tel: 01683 220580
1st right on A701 Edinburgh

2. Craigielands Country Park DG10 9RB
   Tel: 01683 300591
   South end of Beattock Village   ♿

3. Moffat Golf Club DG10 9SB
   Tel: 01683 220020
   A701 Moffat, club signposted on left.

4. Old Brig Inn & Telford Restaurant DG10 9SG
   Tel: 01683 300401
   At r'bout at junction 15   ♿

5. The Pine Tavern DG10 9RD ♿
   South end of Beattock Village ♿

M74 Jn 16

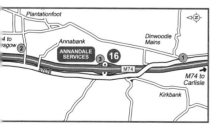

1. Dinwoodie Lodge Hotel DG11 2SL
   Tel: 01576 470289
   B7076 south, on left

2. Red House Hotel DG10 9NF
   Tel: 01576 470470
   B7076 north, 2nd right over motorway

3. Travel Inn DG11 1HD
   Tel: 0870 1977163
   At services

M74 Jn 17

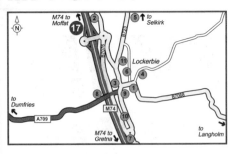

1. The Brig Inn DG11 2HE   ♿
   Tel: 01576 202342
   Exit to Lockerbie, then B7068 to Langholm

2. Dryfesdale Hotel DG11 2SF
   Tel: 01576 202427
   B7076 North

3. Kings Arms Hotel DG11 2JL
   Tel: 01576 202410
   On B7068

4. Lockerbie Golf Club DG11 2ND
   Tel: 01576 203363
   Proceed to Town Centre & follow signs

5. Lockerbie Manor Country Hotel DG11 2RG
   Tel: 01576 202610
   B723 North

6. Lucky Rainbow Chinese Restaurant DG11 2AA
   Tel: 01576 202578
   On B7068

7. Queens Hotel DG11 2RB
   Tel: 01576 202415
   B7076 Lockerbie, on right ♿

8. Ravenshill House Hotel DG11 2EF
   Tel: 01576 202882
   West on A709 Dumfries Road

9. Safeway Supermarket DG11 2BX
   Tel: 01576 204171
   On B7068

10. Somerton House Hotel DG11 2DR
    Tel: 01576 202583
    On Carlisle road, through village

11. Townhead Filling Station DG11 2AG
    Tel: 01576 204280
    On B7068

M74 Jn 19

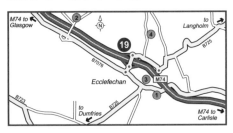

1. Cressfield Country House Hotel DG11 3DR
   Tel: 01576 300281
   South at junction, left, on right

2. Ecclefechan Filling Station DG11 3JB
   Tel: 01576 300622
   B7076 North, right over M74

3. Ecclefechan Post Office and Stores DG11 3DF
   Tel: 01576 300201
   B7076 Ecclefechan, left, left to High St

4. Kirkconnel Hall Hotel DG11 3JH
   Tel: 01576 300277
   Head North at junction, 1st left

SAFETY IN NUMBERS

*voted 'Best Breakdown Provider'
at the 'Your Money' awards 2004*

JOIN THE **SELF PRESERVATION** SOCIETY

greenflag.com

Green Flag
motoring assistance

M8 Summary

No Accessible Facilities **18** **Charing Cross**
0 miles

No Accessible Facilities **17** **Dumbarton A82**
0.5 miles

No Accessible Facilities **16** **St. George's Square**
0.5 miles

No Facilities Listed **15** **Glasgow Cross A803**
1 mile

No Accessible Facilities **14** **Dennistoun B763**
1 mile

No Accessible Facilities **13** **M80**
1 mile

⛽ TTD **12** **Stepps A80** ....*Page 1*
1 mile

No Facilities Listed **11** **Garthamlock B765**
1 mile

☕✕⛽🛒🛏🍷 **10** **Easterhouse** ....*Page 1*
1 mile

No Accessible Facilities **9** **Baillieston**
1 mile

No Accessible Facilities **8** **Edinburgh A8; M73**

M8 becomes A8 for 7 miles

🛏☕✕⛽🛒🍷 **6** **Airdrie A73** ....*Page 1*
5 miles

🛏☕✕🔧⛽🛒🍷 **5** **Shotts B7075** ....*Page 1*
2 miles

⚫ **Harthill Services**
4 miles

🛏☕✕⛽🍷 **4** **Whitburn A801** ....*Page 1*
3 miles

Kwik-Fit 🛏☕✕⛽ TTD 🛒 **3a** **Bathgate A779**...................*Page 1*
3 miles

Kwik-Fit 🛏☕✕🔧⛽ TTD 🛒🍷 **3** **Livingston A899** ....*Page 1*
5 miles

No Accessible Facilities **2** **M9**
4 miles

halfords ☕✕🔧⛽🛒🍷 **1** **City Bypass A720** ....*Page 1*
Total Dist. = 34 miles

🛏️🖥️✕ TTD **31** **Bishopton A8** .... *Page 108*
4 miles

No Accessible Facilities **30** **Erskine M898**
4 miles

🛏️🖥️✕/🍷 **29** **Paisley A726** .... *Page 108*
0.5 miles

No Accessible Facilities **28** **Glasgow Airport**
0.5 miles

🅜 Kwik-Fit 🛏️🖥️✕/⛽🛒🍷 **27** **Renfrew A741** .... *Page 107*
2 miles

🅜 halfords 🛏️🖥️✕/🛒🍷 **26** **Hillington A736** .... *Page 107*
0 miles

No Accessible Facilities **25a** **Braehead**
1 mile

🅜 Kwik-Fit 🖥️✕/⛽🛒🍷 **25** **Clyde Tunnel A761** .... *Page 106*
0.5 miles

🅜 ASDA 🛏️🖥️✕/⛽ TTD 🛒 **24** **Paisley A761** .... *Page 106*
0.5 miles

No Accessible Facilities **23** **Govan B768**
1 mile

No Accessible Facilities **22** **M77**
0 miles

No Accessible Facilities **21** **M77**
1 mile

No Accessible Facilities **20** **East Kilbride (A730)**
1 mile

No Accessible Facilities **19** **Charing Cross**
0 miles

No Accessible Facilities **18** **Charing Cross**
Total Dist. = 16 miles

M8 Jn 1

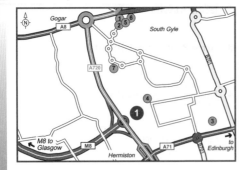

1. Tinos Restaurant EH12 9JR
Tel: 0131 467 2694
A720 North, sharp right at r'bout, on left

2. Burger King EH12 9LH
Tel: 0131 317 1561
A720 North, sharp right at r'bout, on left

3. BP Express Filling Station EH11 4AS
Tel: 0131 458 5419
A720 South, left A71, on left

4. **halfords** HALFORDS EH11 4DF
Tel: 0131 442 2430
A720 South, A71 East, lt at r'bout, 1st lt, on lt

5. Morrison's Supermarket EH12 9JU
Tel: 0131 317 1197
A720 North, sharp right at r'bout, on left

6. Starbucks Coffee EH12 9JY
Tel: 0131 339 3002
A720 North, sharp right at r'bout, on left

7. The Ritz Bar & Grill EH12 9DF
Tel: 0131 317 8800
A720 North, sharp right, right at r'bout

M8 Jn 3

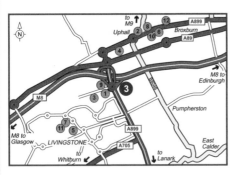

1. B P Deer Park Service Station EH54 8AD
Tel: 01506 434244
On South side of junction

2. Chenzo's Restaurant EH52 5DW
Tel: 01506 855163
On A899

3. Deer Park Golf & Country Club EH54 8AB
Tel: 01506 431037
Right at junction r'bout

4. Houstoun House Hotel & Restaurant EH52 6JS
Tel: 01506 853831
On A899 East

5. **Kwik-Fit** KWIK-FIT EH54 8PT
Tel: 01506 430838
A899 South, right Carmondean Centre

6. Maryville Guest House EH52 5HY
Tel: 01506 856285
On A899 East

7. Safeway Supermarket EH54 8PT
Tel: 01506 433224
A899 South, right Carmondean Centre

8. Co-Op Supermarket EH52 5DZ
Tel: 01506 852109
On A899 East

9. Travel Inn & Deer Park Restaurant EH54 8AD
Tel: 01506 439202
South of junction

10. The Oriental Restaurant EH52 5HY
Tel: 01506 859387
On A899 East

11. The Pentland Inn EH54 8PT
Tel: 01506 436767
A899 South, right Carmondean Centre

12. Somerfield EH52 5JA
Tel: 01506 854835
On A899 East

M8 Jn 3a

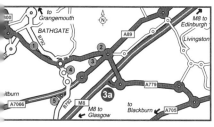

Bathgate Golf Club EH48 IBA
Tel: 01506 630505
North of junction, 2nd exit at r'bout

2. Boghall Filling Station EH48 1LE
Tel: 01506 655494
North of junction, 2nd exit at r'bout

3. Express By Holiday Inn EH48 1LQ
Tel: 01506 650650
On A7066

4. Tesco Supermarket EH48 2ES
Tel: 0845 677 9033
North of junction, 2nd exit at r'bout, left at r'bout

5. Cairn Hotel EH48 2EL
On A7066 West

M8 Jn 4

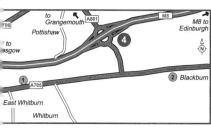

BEST WESTERN HILCROFT HOTEL EH47 0JU
Tel: 01501 740818
Food served all day
Follow signs to Whitburn &

2. Mosshall Service Station EH47 7LX &
Tel: 01506 634215
Left at T-Junction towards Blackburn, situated on right

M8 Jn 5

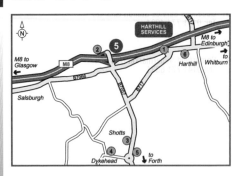

1. Advance Retail Petrol Station ML7 5PT
Tel: 01501 753521
Left at T-junction, B7066

2. Blairmains Guest House ML7 5TJ
Tel: 01501 751278
Just North of junction

3. Fast Fit Tyres & Exhausts Centre ML7 5EP
Tel: 01501 822220
B7057 South

4. Rabellos Italian Restaurant ML7 4BA
Tel: 01501 822050
B7057 South, right Station Rd

5. Shotts Leisure Centre & Pool ML7 5EP
Tel: 01501 823333
B7057 South

6. Co-Op Supermarket ML7 5NL
Tel: 01501 751207
B7066 Harthill

M8 Jn 6

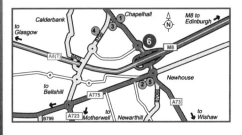

1. Laurel House Inn (Guest House) ML6 8SB
Tel: 01236 763230
On A73 North

2. Travel Inn & Newhouse Restaurant ML1 5SY
Tel: 01698 860277
On A775 West

3. Co-Op Supermarket ML6 8SW
Tel: 01236 762207
A73 North

4. Shawlee Cottage (Guest House) ML6 8SW
Tel: 01236 753774
A73 Chapelhall, left at lights   &

5. BP Express Petrol Station ML1 5SY
Tel: 01698 860236
On A775 West

18 Jn 10

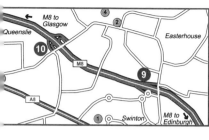

3. Queenslie Service Station G33 4EF
Tel: 0141 774 4004
On A8

4. Somerfield Supermarket G34 9DT
Tel: 0141 771 6331
North from junction

Brewers Fayre G69 6SF
Tel: 0141 773 3494
Exit South, A8 East

Easterhouse Swimming Pool G34 9DU
Tel: 0141 773 4433
North from junction

18 Jn12

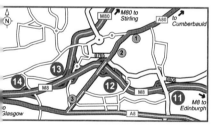

2. Lethamhill Golf Course G33 1AH
Tel: 0141 770 6220
On A80 North

3. Vogue Service Station G33 2EP
Tel: 0141 770 6106
On A80 South

Hogganfield Loch Petrol Station G33 1AE
Tel: 0141 770 4180
On A80 North

M8 Jn 24

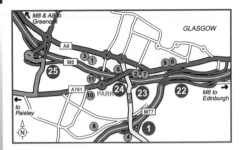

5. Ibrox Service Station G51 2XW
Tel: 0141 427 9903
A8 East, right B768

6. Co-Op Supermarket G51 1BG
Tel: 0141 427 1277
On A8 East

7. Swallow Hotel G51 1RW
Tel: 0141 427 3146
On A761 East

8. The Tea Room Moss Park G52 1JU
Tel: 0141 419 9995
A761 Hillington, left, left, right Airth Dr

9. Walmer Guest House G51 1AT
Tel: 0141 427 0956
A8 East, on left, Walmer Crescent

10. Bellahouston Sports Centre & Pool G52 1HH
A761 West, left Bellahouston Dr

1.	**ASDA GOVAN G51 3HR**
	Tel: 0141 445 4257
	North at junction, on left

2. BP Safeway Store G51 1RP
Tel: 0141 427 4500
A761 East

3. Budget Exhausts & Tyres G51 4XB
Tel: 0141 445 4342
On A8 West

4. Haggs Castle Golf Club G41 4SN
Tel: 0141 427 1157
On B763 South

11.		**MCDONALD'S RESTAURANT G51 3HR**
		Tel: 0141 4453474
	At junction, on Helen Street	

M8 Jn 25

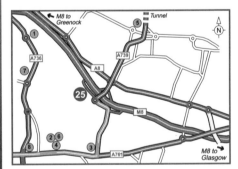

4.	*Kwik-Fit*	**KWIK-FIT G52 3SJ**
	Tel: 0141 883 1790	
	A761 West	

5.		**MCDONALD'S RESTAURANT G51 4JT**
		Tel: 0141 440 1554
	A739 North, left Moss Road	

6. Safeway Supermarket G52 3SQ
Tel: 0141 882 8610
A761 West

7. Shell Petrol Station G52 4BL
Tel: 0141 810 8770
A761 West, A736

8. The Night Palace (Chinese Restaurant) G52 3QH
Tel: 0141 882 3615
A761 West, at cross roads

1. Burger King G52 4BL
Tel: 0141 883 6239
A761 West, A736 North

2. Cardonald Service Station G52 3QA
Tel: 0141 882 1608
A761 West

3. Himalaya Tandoori G52 3TN
Tel: 0141 882 3099
A761 West

18 Jn 26

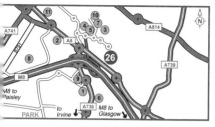

5. Pizza Hut G51 4BS
Tel: 0141 885 9393
Over A8, in Braehead Centre

6. RAC Auto Windscreens G52 4RH
Tel: 0141 882 3322
A736 Hillington, over 1st r'bout, 1st lt, 1st rt.

7. Sainsburys Supermarket G51 4BP
Tel: 0141 886 4541
Over A8, in Braehead Centre

8. Tesco Supermarket PA4 0NQ
Tel: 0845 677 9585
A8 West, 2nd left at r'bout, left Sandy Rd

9. The Hillington (Pub Restaurant) G52 4DR
Tel: 0141 810 1011
A736 South

Burger King G52 4BL
Tel: 0141 883 6239
On A736 South

Dean Park Hotel PA4 8YB
Tel: 0141 886 3771
A8 West, on left

halfords	**HALFORDS** **G51 4BT**

Tel: 0141 885 2701
North at junction, over A8, 1st right

KFC Restaurant G51 4BS
Tel: 0141 886 1698
Over A8, in Braehead Centre

10. | **MCDONALD'S RESTAURANT** 🅿♿ **G51 4BS** ✕⊗ Tel: 0141 8859495
A736 N, straight over r'bout, in Braehead Centre

11. Safeway Supermarket PA4 8QL
Tel: 0141 886 6727
A8 West, on right

18 Jn 27

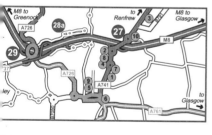

5. Koh-I-Noor Indian Restaurant PA3 2AZ
Tel: 0141 889 7909
A741 South, right A726, right New Sneddon St

6. **Kwik-Fit** **KWIK-FIT** **PA1 1HR**
Tel: 0141 889 9756
A741 South

7. **MCDONALD'S RESTAURANT** **PA3 4DU** Tel: 0141 840 2680 🅿♿ ✕⊗
A741 South

Ardgowan Town House (Guest House) PA3 4BJ
Tel: 0141 889 4763
A741 South, on left ♿

Burger King PA3 4EP
Tel: 0141 889 9532
South of junction, right at r'bout

Glynhill Hotel PA4 8XB
Tel: 0141 886 5555
A741 North

KFC Restaurant PA3 4EA
Tel: 0141 889 1213
A741 South

8. Rockfield Service Station PA3 4EA
Tel: 0141 889 3275
A741 South

9. Safeway Supermarket PA3 2DD
Tel: 0141 889 3286
A741 South, right A726, right Back Sneddon St

10. Shell Petrol Station PA4 8XD
Tel: 0141 842 8900
A741 North of junction

M8 Jn 29

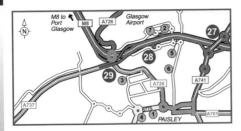

1. Autoglass PA3 1TQ
   Tel: 0141 840 2898
   A726 Paisley, at r'bout rt Underwood Rd

2. Express By Holiday Inn PA3 2TJ
   Tel: 0141 842 1100
   Follow signs to Airport

3. Greenhill House (Guest House) PA3 1RD ♿
   Tel: 0141 889 6752
   A726 South, rt McFarlane St, then Greenhill Rd

4. Mcconechy's Tyre Service Ltd PA1 2PB
   Tel: 0141 889 8881
   A726 South, at r'bout rt Underwood Rd, lt Well St

5. Travel Inn & Slice Restaurant PA3 2TH
   Tel: 0141 842 1563
   Follow signs to Airport, near Terminal Building

6. Dryesdale (Guest House) PA3 2PR
   Tel: 0141 889 7178
   A726 South, left Albion St, left at T-junction

7. The Holiday Inn (Glasgow Airport) PA3 2TE
   Tel: 0870 400 9031
   Follow signs to Airport

M8 Jn 31

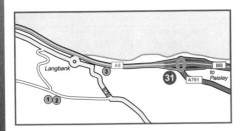

1. Gleddoch Golf Club PA14 6YE
   Tel: 01475 540304
   Left off A8 to B789 East, right Old Greenock Rd

2. Gleddoch House Hotel PA14 6YE
   Tel: 01475 540711
   Left off A8 to B789 East, right Old Greenock Rd

3. Langbank Lodge PA14 6XR
   Tel: 01475 540311
   On Main Road, Langbank

DON'T DRIVE TIRED.

THINK!

M11 Summary

No Accessible Facilities (14) **Huntingdon A14**

2 miles

No Accessible Facilities (13) **Cambridge A1303**

2 miles

🛒✕🛢🛒❗ (12) **Cambridge A603** ....*Page 1*

2 miles

🛏🛒✕🛢🛒❗ (11) **Harston A10, Cambridge** ...*Page 1*

5 miles

[M] 🛏🛒✕🛢(TTD)❗ (10) **Duxford A505** ....*Page 1*

4 miles

No Accessible Facilities (9) **Newmarket A11**

15 miles

🛏🛒✕🔧🛢(TTD)❗ (8) **Bishop's Stortford A120** ....*Page 1*
Birchanger Green Services

10 miles

[M] 🛏🛒✕🛢(TTD)🛒❗ (7) **Harlow A414** .... *Page 1*

4 miles

No Accessible Facilities (6) **M25**

4 miles

No Accessible Facilities (5) **Loughton A1168**

4 miles

No Accessible Facilities (4) **North Circular Road A406**

Total Dist. **= 52 miles**

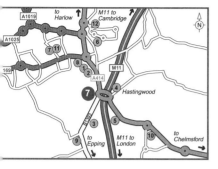

Little Chef CM17 9YP
Tel: 01279 417057
A414 Harlow, on left

Shell Garage
Tel: 01279 635980
A414 Harlow, on left

MCDONALD'S RESTAURANT CM17 9LH
Tel: 01279 454367
B1393 Epping, on left

4. Rainbow & Dove Restaurant CM17 9JX
Tel: 01279 415419
A414 Chelmsford, 1st left, on left

5. Harlow Garden Centre CM17 9LD
Tel: 01279 419039
A414 Chelmsford, on right

6. The Gatekeeper Beefeater Restaurant CM17 9DX
Tel: 01279 424495
A414 Harlow, right London Rd

7. Garden of India (Restaurant) CM18 6PA
Tel: 01279 430942
A414 North, lt at r'bout, rt Tawneys Rd, 2nd rt

8. Harlow (Stansted) Moat House CM18 7BA
Tel: 01279 829988
On A414 North

9. Neales Garage (Petrol) CM16 6LX
Tel: 01992 572017
B1393 South

10. North Weald Golf Club CM16 6AR
01992 522118
A414 Chelmsford

11. Paklock Chinese Restaurant CM18 6NZ
01279 425739
A414 North, lt at r'bout, rt Tawneys Rd, 2nd rt

12. Tesco Supermarket CM17 9TE
0845 677 9332
A414 North, right at 3rd r'bout

M11 Jn 8

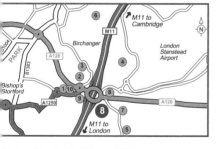

Bishops Stortford Golf Course CM23 5
Tel: 01622 734322
A120 West, left at r'bout

The Stansted Manor Hotel CM23 5ST
Tel: 01279 859800
A120 Standon, 3rd exit at r'bout, on left &

The Three Willows CM23 5QR
Tel: 01279 815913
A120 Standon, 3rd exit at r'bout &

Hilton London Stansted Airport CM24 1SF
Tel: 01279 680800
Follow signs to Standsted Airport &

5. The Hop Poles Pub & Restaurant CM22 7TP
Tel: 01279 757042
A120 East, 1st right, on left

6. Mountfitchet Castle and Norman Village CM24 8SP
Tel: 01279 813237
A120 Standon, 3rd exit of 2nd r'bout, on right

7. Great Hallingbury Manor (Guest House) CM22 7TJ
Tel: 0800 032 1066
A120 East, 1st right

8. Start Hill Service Station CM22 7TA
Tel: 01279 503959
Old A120 East

9. Welcome Lodge CM23 5QZ
Tel: 01279 656477
At Birchanger Green Services

10. Partco Autoparts Ltd CM23 5PJ
Tel: 01279 657827
A120 West, lt at r'bout, rt Parsonage La, 3rd lt

M11 Jn 10

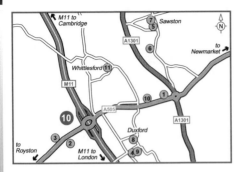

1. **MCDONALD'S RESTAURANT
CB2 4HD**
Tel: 01223 836947
A505 Pampisford, 2 miles, at r'bout

2. Imperial War Museum CB2 4QR
Tel: 01223 835000
A505 West, on left

3. Duxford Service Station CB2 4QQ
Tel: 01223 832412
A505 West, on right

4. Duxford Lodge Hotel CB2 4RT
Tel: 01223 836444
A505 East, 1st right

5. Jade Fountain Restaurant CB2 4BG
Tel: 01223 836100
A505 East, left at r'bout, into Sawston

6. South Cambridgeshire Guest House CB2 4EF
Tel: 01223 834523
A505 East, left at r'bout, right Sawston

7. The Greyhound CB2 4BG
Tel: 01223 832260
A505 East, left at r'bout, right Sawston

8. The John Barleycorn CB2 4PP
Tel: 01223 832699
A505 East, 2nd right Duxford

9. The Plough CB2 4RP
Tel: 01223 833170
A505 East, right Duxford, left St Peters St

10. The Red Lion Hotel CB2 4NL
Tel: 01223 832047
A505 East, signs on left

11. Tickell Arms CB2 4NZ
Tel: 01223 833128
A505 East, 3rd left Whittlesford

M11 Jn 11

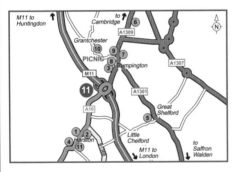

1. Harston Service Station CB2 5QB
Tel: 01223 872287
A10 Harston, on right

2. The Old English Gentleman CB2 5QD
Tel: 01223 870287
A10 Harston, on left

3. Waitrose Superstore CB2 2LQ
Tel: 01223 845777
A1309 Trumpington, on left

4. Crayfish Restaurant & Oyster Bar CB2 5PX
Tel: 01223 870349
A10 Harston, on right

5. Chef Peking CB2 5LZ
Tel: 01223 843089
A1309 Trumpington, right A1301

6. Meadowcroft Hotel CB2 2EX
Tel: 01223 346120
A1309 Cambridge, on right

7. Out And Out Restaurant & Bar CB2 2HZ
Tel: 01223 844903
A1309 Cambridge, on right

8. Shell Petrol Station CB2 2LS
Tel: 01223 846990
A1309 Trumpington, on left

9. The Coach & Horses CB2 2LP
Tel: 01223 506248
A1309 Trumpington, on left

10. The Orchard Tea Gardens CB3 9ND
Tel: 01223 845788
A1309 Trumpington, left Grantchester

11. The Pemberton Arms CB2 5PX
Tel: 01223 870351
A10 Harston, on left

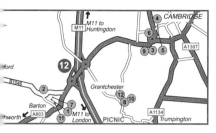

The White Horse Inn CB3 7BG
Tel: 01223 262327
A603 Barton, right High St

The Hoops Public House CB3 7BD
Tel: 01223 262230
A603 Barton, right to B1046

Co-op Supermarket CB3 9HY
Tel: 01223 361425
A603 Cambridge, right Granchester St

India House Restaurant CB3 9EY
Tel: 01223 461661
A603 Cambridge, on right after r'bout

5. Sala Thong Thai Restaurant CB3 9EY
Tel: 01223 323178
A603 Cambridge, on right after r'bout

6. Shell Petrol Station CB3 9EY
Tel: 01223 450000
A603 Cambridge, at r'bout

7. The Barn Tea Rooms CB3 7BD
Tel: 01223 264821
A603 Barton, right New Rd, left School Lane

8. The Green Man CB3 9NF
Tel: 01223 841178
Take Granchester exit at r'bout

9. The Red Bull CB3 9JZ
Tel: 01223 300943
A603 Cambridge

10. The Red Lion CB3 9NF
Tel: 01223 840121
Take Granchester exit at r'bout

11. The White Horse CB3 7BG
Tel: 01223 262327
A603 Barton, right High St

12. The Rupert Brooke Restaurant CB3 9NQ
Tel: 01223 840295
Take Granchester exit at r'bout

M20 Summary

ASDA ⬛✕⛽🚻🛒	**1**	**M25; Swanley B2173** .... *Page 1*
		7 miles
No Accessible Facilities	**2**	**Wrotham A20**
		3 miles
No Accessible Facilities	**3**	**M26**
		3 miles
🛏⬛✕⛽🛒🍷	**4**	**West Malling A228** .... *Page 1*
		3 miles
halfords 🛏⬛✕🔧⛽🚻🛒🍷	**5/6**	**Aylesford A20** .... *Page 1*
		2 miles
🛏⬛✕🛒🍷	**7**	**Maidstone A249** .... *Page 1*
		4 miles
🛏⬛✕⛽🚻🛒🍷	**8**	**Lenham A20, Bearsted** ...... *Page 1*
		Maidstone Services
		13 miles
Ⓜ *Kwik-Fit* **halfords** 🛏⬛✕🔧🛒	**9**	**Ashford A20** .... *Page 1*
		2 miles
Ⓜ ⬛✕🔧🛒🍷	**10**	**Brenzett A2070** .... *Page 1*
		7 miles
🛏⬛✕🔧⛽🚻🛒🍷	**11**	**Canterbury B2068/A20** ...... *Page 1*
		3 miles
No Accessible Facilities	**11a**	**Channel Tunnel**
		1 mile
Kwik-Fit ⬛✕🔧⛽🛒🍷	**12**	**Cheriton A20** .... *Page 1*
		1 mile
Ⓜ **halfords** 🛏⬛✕🔧🛒	**13**	**Folkestone A20** .... *Page 1*
		Total Dist. **= 49 miles**

WEST ⬆

M25

1. **ASDA** ASDA SWANLEY
BR8 7UN
Tel: 01322 668526
B2173 Swanley

China Red Restaurant BR8 8AE
Tel: 01322 666663
B2173 Swanley

3. Fuelforce Petrol Station BR8 8AF
Tel: 01322 662955
B2173 Swanley

4. Pedham Place Golf Centre BR8 8PP
Tel: 01322 867000
A20 East

5. Premier Chinese Restaurant BR8 8ES
Tel: 01322 665115
B2173 Swanley, left Station Rd

6. Raj Of India Restaurant BR8 8AE
Tel: 01322 613651
B2173 Swanley

7. The Chef Chinese Restaurant BR8 7TQ
Tel: 01322 665432
B2173 Swanley

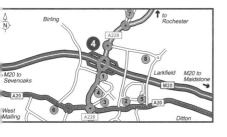

Travel Inn & Brewsters ME19 5TR
Tel: 08701 977170
A228 South, on left.

Tesco Express ME20 6HJ
A228 South, left at lights, on left

Parkfoot Garage Petrol Station ME19 5EY
Tel: 01732 840159
A228 South, left at lights, on left

4. The Old Rectory Restaurant ME19 5PU
Tel: 01732 844888
A228 South, on left in Leybourne

5. Larkfield Priory Hotel ME20 6HJ
Tel: 0870 609 6157
A228 South, left A20, on left

6. Parkfoot Garage Petrol Station ME19 5AE
Tel: 01732 840000
A228 South, right A20

7. Shell Petrol Station ME6 5LB
Tel: 01634 247920
A228 North, on left

8. Tesco Supermarket & Petrol Station ME20 6RJ
Tel: 0845 677 9445
A228 North, right at r'bout, on right

M20 Jn 5/6

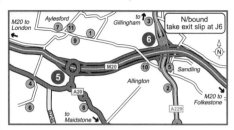

1. ATS Euromaster ME20 7SB
   Tel: 01622 715737
   From South of J6 take Forstal Rd

2. Chatham Road Service Station ME14 2ND
   Tel: 01622 683597
   On A229 South

3. Cobtree Manor Park Golf Course ME14 3AZ
   Tel: 01622 753276
   From J6 take A229 North

4. **halfords** HALFORDS ME20 7TP
   Tel: 01622 715333
   From J5 take A20 West

5. Running Horse Harvester Restaurant ME14 3AG
   Tel: 01622 752975
   From J6 take A229 South

6. Sainsburys Supermarket ME20 7NA
   Tel: 01622 790223
   From J5 take A20 West, left Mills Rd

7. Sherlocks Restaurant ME20 7BA
   Tel: 01622 710649
   From J5 take A20 West, rt Hall Rd, rt Station Rd

8. Sir Thomas Wyatt Restaurant ME16 0HG
   Tel: 01622 752515
   From J5 take A20 East

9. The Hengist Restaurant ME20 7AX
   Tel: 01622 719273
   From South of J6 take Forstal Rd

10. Travel Inn & Malta Inn Restaurant ME14 3AS
    Tel: 0870 197 7308
    From South of J6 take Forstal Rd

11. Wickham Lodge Guest House ME20 7AY
    Tel: 01622 717267
    At J5 A20 W, rt Hall Rd, rt Station Rd, lt High St

M20 Jn 7

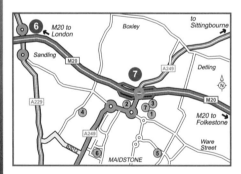

1. Newnham Court Shopping Village ME14 5LH
   Tel: 01252 408820
   A249 south, left at r'bout, on left

2. Hilton (Maidstone) ME14 5AA
   Tel: 01622 734322
   A249 south, right at r'bout, on right

3. Noble House Restaurant ME15 8XW
   Tel: 01622 863168
   A249 S, lt at r'bout, on lt (Newnham Ct Village)

4. Russell Hotel ME14 2AE
   Tel: 01622 692221
   A249 South, right at 2 r'bout, left at r'bout

5. Tesco Supermarket ME14 5TQ
   Tel: 0845 677 9447
   A249 S, lt at r'bt, rt at r'bt, lt at r'bt, on rt

6. Vinters Park Indian Cuisine ME14 5NS
   Tel: 01622 756633
   A249 S, lt Claremont Rd, rt, lt, lt Snowdon Parade

7. Coffee Corner ME14 5EL
   Tel: 01622 736744
   A249 S, lt at r'bout, on lt (Newnham Ct Village)

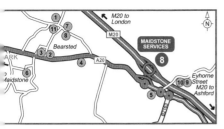

5. Ramada Hotel & Resort ME17 1RE
   Tel: 01622 632379
   A20 East

6. Somerfield Supermarket ME15 8LH
   Tel: 01622 739981
   A20 Maidstone, left Spot La, 1st right, 1st left

7. Souffle Restaurant On The Green ME14 4DN
   Tel: 01622 737065
   A20 Maidstone, right Bearsted

8. The Oak On The Green ME14 4EJ
   Tel: 01622 737976
   A20 Maidstone, right Bearsted

9. The Sugar Loaves (Public House) ME17 1TS
   Tel: 01622 880220
   A20 East, left at r'bout for Hollingbourne

10. The Windmill (Public House) ME17 1TR
    Tel: 01622 880280
    A20 East, left at r'bout for Hollingbourne

11. White Horse Beefeater ME14 4DL
    Tel: 01622 738365
    A20 Maidstone, right Bearsted

- Bearsted Golf Club ME14 4PQ
  Tel: 01622 738389
  A20 Maidstone, right Bearsted

- Bearsted Service Station ME14 4NE
  Tel: 01622 737678
  A20 Maidstone

- Kentish Yeoman (Public House) ME14 4BT
  Tel: 01622 737744
  A20 Maidstone, on right

- Marriott Tudor Park Hotel & Country Club ME14 4NQ
  Tel: 01622 739412
  A20 Maidstone, on left

M20 Jn 9

5. **MCDONALD'S RESTAURANT TN24 8TE**
   Tel: 01233 647445
   A292 East, right Station Rd, right High St

6. Sainsburys Supermarket TN24 8YN
   Tel: 01233 610841
   South of junction at exit

7. The Bybrook Barn Harvester TN24 8QQ
   Tel: 01233 663634
   Take A20 East, then A28 North

8. Travelodge TN25 4BN
   Tel: 01233 624213
   North of junction in Eureka Leisure Park

9. Burger King TN25 4BN
   North of junction in Eureka Leisure Park

- Ashford International Hotel TN24 8UX
  Tel: 01233 219988
  South of junction, on A20

- Haysbank Guest House TN24 8JX
  Tel: 01233 627573
  A292 East, left Canterbury Rd

- KFC Restaurant TN25 4BN
  Tel: 01233 663138
  North of junction in Eureka Leisure Park

4. **KWIK-FIT TN24 8PE**
   Tel: 01233 632577
   A292 East

10. **HALFORDS TN24 8XH**
    South of junction

11. Pizza Hut TN25 4BN
    North of junction in Eureka Leisure Park

M20 Jn 10

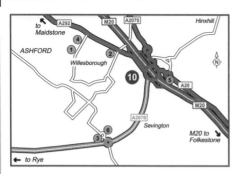

3. **MCDONALD'S RESTAURANT TN24 0TA**
Tel: 01233 503587
A2070 South, right at r'bout, on left

4. TC's Tyres & Exhausts TN24 0RS
Tel: 01233 631286
A292, left Hunter Rd, right Glover Rd

5. Tesco Supermarket TN24 0YE
Tel: 0845 677 9008
A20 South, on right

6. Travel Inn and Brewers Fayre TN24 0GN
Tel: 0870 1977305
A2070, on right

1. Co-Op Supermarket TN24 0HG
Tel: 01233 621339
A292, left Hunter Rd

2. Dickinsons Café TN24 0QL
Tel: 01233 623969
A292, on left

M20 Jn 11

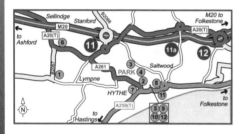

6. The Airport Café TN25 6DA
Tel: 01303 813185
Take directions A20 Sellindge

7. The Light Railway Restaurant CT21 6LD
Tel: 01303 266419
A20 South, left A261, over river

8. The Rowan Tree French Restaurant CT21 5JT
Tel: 01303 267912
A20 South, left A261, on A259

9. The Swan Hotel CT21 5AD
Tel: 01303 266236
A20 South, left A261, on A259

10. Vinodham Tandoori CT21 5AL
Tel: 01303 230797
A20 South, left A261, on A259

11. Waitrose Supermarket CT21 5NH
Tel: 01303 230318
A20 South, left A261, on A259

12. White Hart (Guest House) CT21 5AJ
Tel: 01303 263121
A20 South, left A261, on A259

1. ATS Euromaster CT21 4LR
Tel: 01303 237889
A20 South, left B2067

2. BP Petrol Station CT21 5DD
Tel: 01303 265362
A20 South, left A261

3. Brockhill Country Park CT21 4HL
Tel: 01303 266327
A20 North, 1st right

4. Castle Hotel CT21 4AJ
Tel: 01303 266311
A20 North, 1st right

5. Sotirios Restaurant CT21 5NS
Tel: 01303 262000
A20 South, left A261, on A259

M20 Jn 12

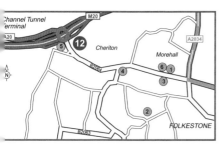

4. The Prince Of India CT19 4JH
Tel: 01303 276298
B2064 Folkestone, on right

5. Tesco Supermarket CT19 4QJ
Tel: 0845 677 9273
B2064, first right, on right

6. Total Petrol Station CT19 4DP
Tel: 01303 298600
B2064, on left

ATS Euromaster CT19 4DP
Tel: 01303 275198
B2064, on left

Gurkha Palace Restaurant CT20 3NE
Tel: 01303 259900
B2064, rt Risborough Ln, lt Shorncliffe Rd, rt Ernbrook Valley

3. **Kwik-Fit** KWIK-FIT CT19 4AZ
Tel: 01303 275906
B2064, on right

M20 Jn 13

4. Sainsburys Supermarket CT19 5GA
Tel: 01303 850810
A259, right at r'bout

5. Travel Inn & Brewsters CT19 4AP
Tel: 0870 197 7103
A2034, right at lights, on right

6. **halfords** HALFORDS CT19 5DS
Tel: 01303 251101
A259, right at r'bout

1. **MCDONALD'S RESTAURANT CT19 5GA**
Tel: 01303 249256
A259, right at r'bout

Partco Autoparts Ltd CT19 5DS
Tel: 01303 241156
A259, on right

Safeway Supermarket CT19 5JS
Tel: 01303 251587
A2034, left, on left

SAFETY IN NUMBERS

*voted 'Best Breakdown Provider'
at the 'Your Money' awards 2004*

JOIN THE **SELF PRESERVATION** SOCIETY ➜

greenflag.com

Green Flag
motoring assistance

A member of the General Insurance Standards Council

M62 Summary

 🅵⛽✕🚿🛏️🍴 **19** **Middleton; Heywood A6046** *page 127*

1 mile

Birch Services

2 miles

Continues as M62

No Accessible Facilities **18** **M66/M60**

2 miles

 🔧✕🚿🛏️🍴⛽ **17** **Whitefield A56** .... *page 126*

2 miles

No Accessible Facilities **16** **Swinton A666**

1 mile

No Accessible Facilities **15** **M61**

1 mile

No Accessible Facilities **14** **St Helens A580**

2 miles

🛏️🍴⛽✕🍴 **13** **Swinton A572** .... *page 126*

1 mile

No Accessible Facilities **12** **M60/M62**

7 miles

M62 becomes M60 from J12 to J18

 **ASDA** 🔧🛒🍴✕⛽🍴 **11** **Birchwood A574** .... *page 125*

2 miles

No Accessible Facilities **10** **M6**

1 mile

 ⛽🛏️🍴✕🍴 **9** **Warrington A49** .... *page 125*

3 miles

Burtonwood Services

0 miles

 🛒🍴✕⛽🍴 **8** **Burtonwood A574** .... *page 124*

4 miles

🛏️🍴✕🍴 **7** **St Helens A570** .... *page 124*

3 miles

✕🛏️🍴⛽🍴 **6** **M57/Runcorn A5300** .... *page 123*

3 miles

 **ASDA** 🛒🛏️🍴✕(TTD)🍴 **5** **Huyton A5080** .... *page 123*

1 mile

No Facilities Listed **4** **Liverpool A5058**

Total Dist. = 36 miles

EAST

M62 Liverpool to Middleton

121

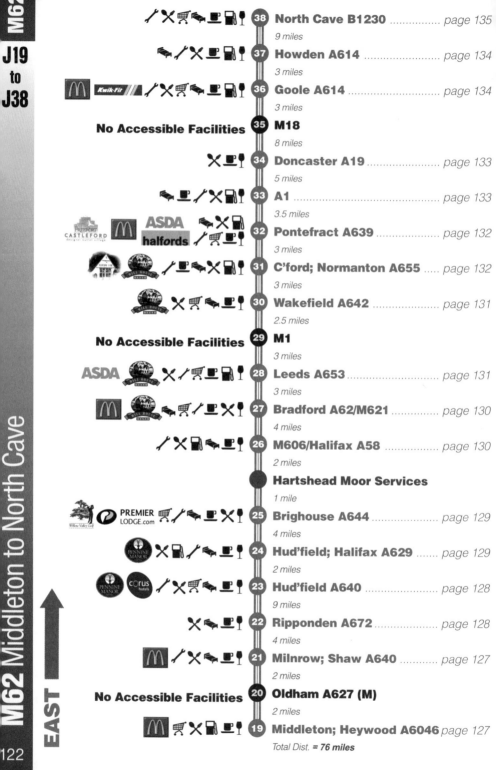

Facilities	Jct	Destination	Page
🔧✕🛒🐟☕⛽🍷	38	**North Cave B1230**	*page 135*
		9 miles	
🛏️🔧✕☕⛽	37	**Howden A614**	*page 134*
		3 miles	
Ⓜ Kwik-Fit 🔧✕🛒🐟☕🍴🍷	36	**Goole A614**	*page 134*
		3 miles	
No Accessible Facilities	35	**M18**	
		8 miles	
✕☕🍷	34	**Doncaster A19**	*page 133*
		5 miles	
🐟☕🔧✕⛽🍷	33	**A1**	*page 133*
		3.5 miles	
FREEPORT CASTLEFORD Ⓜ ASDA halfords 🐟✕🔧🛒⛽🍷	32	**Pontefract A639**	*page 132*
		3 miles	
🏠 🦉 🔧☕🛏️✕⛽🍷	31	**C'ford; Normanton A655**	*page 132*
		3 miles	
🦉 ✕🛒🛏️☕🍷	30	**Wakefield A642**	*page 131*
		2.5 miles	
No Accessible Facilities	29	**M1**	
		3 miles	
ASDA 🦉 ✕🔧🛒☕⛽🍷	28	**Leeds A653**	*page 131*
		3 miles	
Ⓜ 🦉 🐟🛒🔧☕✕🍷	27	**Bradford A62/M621**	*page 130*
		4 miles	
🔧✕⛽🐟☕🍷	26	**M606/Halifax A58**	*page 130*
		2 miles	
	⚫	**Hartshead Moor Services**	
		1 mile	
Willow Valley Golf 🅿 PREMIER LODGE.com 🛒🔧🐟☕✕🍷	25	**Brighouse A644**	*page 129*
		4 miles	
PENNINE MANOR ✕⛽🔧🐟☕🍷	24	**Hud'field; Halifax A629**	*page 129*
		2 miles	
PENNINE MANOR corus hotels 🔧✕🛒🐟☕🍷	23	**Hud'field A640**	*page 128*
		9 miles	
✕🐟☕🍷	22	**Ripponden A672**	*page 128*
		4 miles	
Ⓜ 🔧✕🐟☕🍷	21	**Milnrow; Shaw A640**	*page 127*
		2 miles	
No Accessible Facilities	20	**Oldham A627 (M)**	
		2 miles	
Ⓜ 🛒✕⛽☕🍷	19	**Middleton; Heywood A6046**	*page 127*

Total Dist. = 76 miles

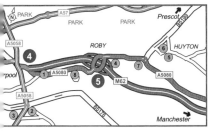

5. **MCDONALD'S RESTAURANT**
L36 5RT
Tel: 0151 4490237
A5080 Huyton, left on B5199, 4th right

6. **ASDA SUPERMARKET**
L36 9YE
Tel: 0151 4808540
A5080 Huyton, 1st exit at r'bout, on right

The Turnpike Tavern L14 3PL
Tel: 0151 7382921
A5080 Knotty Ash, on left after two lights

Childwall Fiveways Public House L15 6XS
Tel: 0151 7223314
A5058 Mossley Hill, on left after r'bout

Owens Restaurant L15 6XX
Tel: 0151 7223845
A5058 Mossley Hill, on right after r'bout

Premier Lodge & Henry's Table L36 4HD
Tel: 0870 9906596
A5080 Huyton, on right

7. The Crofters Arms L36 4HD
Tel: 0151 4824951
A5080 Huyton, on right

8. National Wildflower Centre L16 3NA
Tel: 0151 7371819
A5080 Liverpool, signposted

162 Jn 6

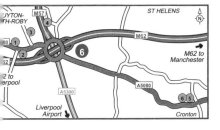

The Hare & Hounds Public House L35 1QJ
Tel: 0151 4893046
A5080 West, on right

Woodlands Petrol Station L35
Tel: 0151 4806284
A5080 West, on left

Travel Inn & Brewsters L36 6AD
Tel: 08701 977159
A5080 West, 1st right

4. The Village Hotel & Leisure Club L35 1RZ
Tel: 0151 4492341
200m from junction

5. The Black Horse Inn WA8 5QG
Tel: 0151 4242965
A5080 Cronton, left at lights

6. The Unicorn Inn WA8 5QF
Tel: 0151 4951304
A5080 Cronton, on left

M62 Jn 7

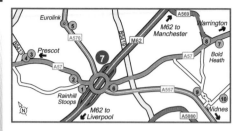

1. Rainhill Motors L35 6PF
   Tel: 0151 4264199
   A57 West, on left

2. Premier Lodge & Henry's Table L35 6PE
   Tel: 0870 9906446
   A57 West, on left

3. The Victoria Public House L35 0LR
   Tel: 0151 4263694
   A57 West, on right

4. Manolitos Italian/Mexican Restaurant L35 0LR
   Tel: 0151 4309212
   Take A57 West, on right

5. Travel Inn & Brewsters WA9 4TT
   Tel: 08701 977237
   A570 North, on right

6. Harefield Cottage Water Gardens L35 6PG
   Tel: 0151 4306647
   A57 Warrington, on right

7. The Griffin Inn WA8 3XT
   Tel: 0151 4245143
   A57 Warrington, on right

8. Maplewood Cantonese Restaurant WA8 3UX
   Tel: 0151 4242259
   A57 Warrington, on left

9. Rivendell Garden Centre & Restaurant WA8 3UL
   Tel: 01744 750606
   A557 Widnes, first left, left at r'bout, on left

10. Everglades Park Hotel WA8 3UJ
    Tel: 0151 4952040
    A557 Widnes, first left, right at r'bout, left at r'bout, on right

M62 Jn 8

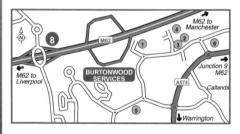

1. Marks & Spencer WA5 7WG
   Tel: 01925 710077
   Follow signposts for Gemini Retail Park

2. Ikea WA5 7WG
   Follow signposts for Gemini Retail Park

3. **MCDONALD'S RESTAURANT WA5 5WG**
   Tel: 01925 574595
   Follow signposts for Gemini Retail Park

4. Boots WA5 7TY
   Tel: 01925 658934
   Follow signposts for Gemini Retail Park

5. Memphis Belle Pub WA5 8WF
   Tel: 01925 712173
   Follow signposts for Gemini Retail Park

6. BP Petrol Station WA5 7TT
   Tel: 01925 710067
   Follow signposts for Gemini Retail Park

162 Jn 9

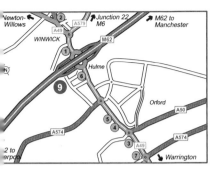

Burger King Restaurant WA2 8ID
Tel: 01925 573387
A49 Newton-le-Willows, first left

Premier Lodge & Swan Tavern WA2 8LF
Tel: 0870 9906620
A49 Newton-le-Willows, through 2 lights, on right after r'bout

3. BP Petrol Station
A49 Warrington, on right at 2nd r'bout

4. KFC Restaurant WA2 8TW
Tel: 01925 419786
A49 Warrington, right at 2nd r'bout, Alban Retail Park

5. Pizza Hut Restaurant WA2
Tel: 01925 574220
A49 Warrington, right at 2nd r'bout, Alban Retail Park

6. Travel Inn & Brewers Fayre WA2 8RN
Tel: 01925 414417
A49 Warrington, on right

7.		**MCDONALD'S RESTAURANT WA2 8HQ** Tel: 01925 444989	💻♿ ✕⊗

A49 Warrington, on right after 2nd r'about

162 Jn 11

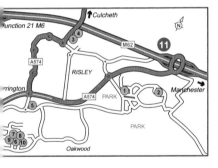

The Poacher Inn WA3 6TS
Tel: 01925 831942
A574 Birchwood, left at 2 r'bouts, on left

Spar Food Store WA3 6UG
Tel: 01925 811090
A574 Birchwood, left at 2 r'bouts, left at fork, on right

The Noggin Inn & Henry's Table Restaurant WA3 6AX
Tel: 01925 812022
A574 Birchwood, right at r'bout, right at 3rd r'bout, on right

S.R. Williams Garage WA3 6AY
Tel: 01925 816700
A574 Birchwood, right at r'bout, right at 3rd r'bout, on right

5. Oakwood Gate Petrol Station WA3 6RW
Tel: 01925 827300
A574 Birchwood, at 2nd r'bout turn left, on left

6.	**ASDA**	**ASDA SUPERMARKET WA3 7PG** Tel: 01925 823601	💻£ ✕♿ HGV⊗ ⛽

A574 Birchwood, follow signs for Birchwood Shopping Centre

7. Artisan Café Bar WA3 7PG
Tel: 01925 825725
A574 Birchwood, follow signs for Birchwood Shopping Centre

8.		**MCDONALD'S RESTAURANT WA3 7PQ** Tel: 01925 850729	💻♿ ✕⊗

A574 Birchwood, follow signs for Birchwood Shopping Centre

9. Birchwood Shopping Centre WA3 7PG
Tel: 01925 822411
A574 Birchwood, follow signs for Birchwood Shopping Centre

10. Birchwood Leisure Centre WA3 7PQ
Tel: 01925 458130
A574 Birchwood, follow signs for Birchwood Shopping Centre

M62 (M60) Jn 13

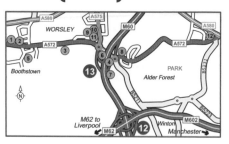

1. Marco Polo Italian Restaurant M28 1FB
Tel: 0161 7901427
A572 Boothstown, on right

2. Shabaaz Indian Restaurant M28 1FB
Tel: 0161 7908505
A572 Boothstown, on right

3. Worsley Hall Garden Centre M28 2LJ
Tel: 0161 7908792
A572 Boothstown, on left

4. **JOHN GILBERT PUB/RESTAURANT**
Tel: 0161 7037733 **M28 2YA**
Trad. English pub food served daily
Situated at junction

5. Millers Pub & Restaurant M28 1YB
Tel: 0161 7026251
A580 Boothstown, on left

6. Novotel Hotel M28 2YA
Tel: 0161 7993535
Situated at junction

7. Milan Italian Restaurant M28 2PD
Tel: 0161 7945444
B5211 Eccles, on right

8. Café Bar Rioja M28 2NL
Tel: 0161 7936003
A572 Pendlebury, on left

9. Marriott Worsley Park Hotel & Country Club M28 2(
Tel: 0161 9752000
A575 Worsley, on left

10. Worsley Petrol Station M28 2
Tel: 0161 7020370
A575 Worsley, on left

11. Worsley Old Hall Pub/Rest. M28 2QT
Tel: 0161 7992960
A575 Worsley, on left

12. Premier Lodge & Millers Kitchen M27 0AA
Tel: 0161 7282791
A572 Pendlebury, left onto A580, on left

M62 (M60) Jn 17

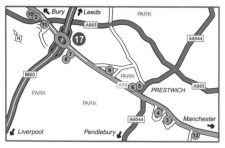

1. **MOBILE AUTOCARE LTD M27 8SF**
Anytime 0161 7949994
Auto elec fault finding/repairs/breakdown
Not on map - off junction 16

2. Akrams Eastern Cuisine M45 7ET
Tel: 0161 7960403
A56 Whitefield, on left

3. The Village Hotel & Leisure Club M25 9WS
Tel: 0161 7988905
A56 Prestwich, on right by KFC

4. KFC Fastfood Restaurant M25 9NQ
Tel: 0161 7734056
A56 Prestwich, on right

5. The Friendship Inn M25 0PD
Tel: 0161 7732645
A56 Prestwich, left at lights

6. Saporito Ristorante Pizzeria M25 0PD
Tel: 0161 773 0700
A56 Prestwich, left at lights

7. Travel Inn & TGI Fridays M25 3AJ
Tel: 08701 977175
A56 Prestwich, on right close to junction

8. Tesco Supermarket M25 3TG
Tel: 0161 9109400
A56 Prestwich, on right close to junction

9. BP Petrol Station M25 1AR
Tel: 0161 772 9969
A56 Prestwich, on left

10. Khan Saab Indian Restaurant M25 6AA
Tel: 0161 7662148
A56 Whitefield, on left

11. **MCDONALD'S RESTAURANT
M45 7EG**
Tel: 0161 7679731
A56 Whitefield, on left

12. **THE HAZELDEAN HOTEL M7 3NE**
Tel: 0161 792 6667/2079
High quality service, friendly atmosphere
A56 Prestwich, on right after lights

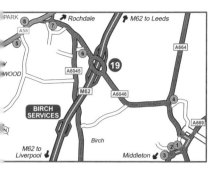

3. Middleton Archer Public House M24 4AA
Tel: 0161 6539721
A6046 South, right at r'bout

4. The White Hart Inn M24 2QA
Tel: 0161 6435529
A664 South, on right

5. The Crown Inn OL10 3HH
Tel: 01706 360270
A6046 Heywood, left to A58, on left

6. Texaco Star Mart OL10 2
Tel: 01706 360557
A6046 Heywood, on left

 MCDONALD'S RESTAURANT
M24 4DF
Tel: 0161 6554193
A6046 Manchester, right at r'bout

7. Piccolo's Italia OL10 1LJ
Tel: 01706 365561
A6046 Heywood, on left

Middleton Shopping Centre M24 4EL
Tel: 0161 6434900
A6046 South, right at r'bout

8. Morrisons Superstore OL10 4PU
Tel: 01706 360036
A6046 Heywood, left to A58, on right

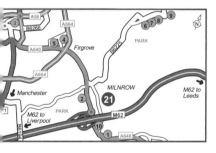

5. Newbold Tyres & Exhausts
Tel: 01706 353144
A640 North, on right

6. Hollingworth Lake Water Activity Centre OL15 0DQ
Tel: 01706 370499
A640 North, follow signs for Hollingworth Lake

7. RISTORANTE DEL LAGO OL15 0DQ
Tel: 01706 376587
Specialise in fresh fish and shellfish
A640 North, follow signs for Hollingworth Lake

Newhey Garage OL16 3RU
Tel: 01706 882431
A640 South, on left

The Ladybarn Hungry Horse OL16 4HF
Tel: 01706 355402
A640 North, on left

8. The Singing Kettle Tea Room OL15 0DQ
Tel: 01706 379094
A640 North, follow signs for Hollingworth Lake

9. The Fisherman's Inn OL15 0AZ
Tel: 01706 378168
A640 North, follow signs for Hollingworth Lake

 MCDONALDS RESTAURANT
OL16 1JW
Tel: 01706 350443
A640 Rochdale, B6223, left B6226, right r'bout, on right

10. Travel Inn & Brewers Fayre OL16 4JF
Tel: 08701 977219
A640 South, on left at junction

KFC Restaurant OL16 5AF
Tel: 01706 647618
A640 North, right to A664, on left

M62 Jn 22

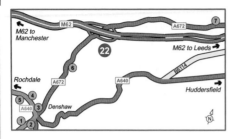

4. **LA PERGOLA HOTEL & RESTAURANT OL3 5U**
   Tel: 01457 871040
   Friendly, family-run hotel, best food & wine
   A672 Denshaw, right onto A640, on right

5. Alpine Restaurant OL3 5UE
   Tel: 01457 874254
   A672 Denshaw, after 2 miles right at junction, on left

6. The Ramshead Inn OL3 5UN
   Tel: 01457 874802
   A672 Denshaw, on left

7. The Turnpike Inn HX6 4QT
   Tel: 01422 822789
   A672 East, on left

1. The Printer's Arms OL3 5SN
   Tel: 01457 874248
   A672 Denshaw, on right

2. The Black Horse Inn OL3 5SL
   Tel: 01457 874375
   A672 Denshaw, on left

3. The Junction Inn OL3 5SE
   Tel: 01457 874265
   A672 Denshaw, after 2 miles right at junction, on right

M62 Jn 23

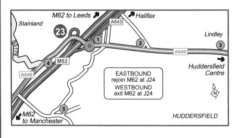

4. **OLD GOLF HOUSE HOTEL & REST.**
   Tel: 01422 379311   **HD3 3YP**
   52 beds/rest/bar/
   pitch & putt/free park.
   A640 South, on left

   cοrus hotels

5. **PENNINE MANOR HOTEL & REST.**
   Tel: 01484 642368   **HD7 4NH**
   Ideally placed for
   business/pleasure
   A640 South, through Outlane, first left

   PENNINE MANOR HOTEL

1. The Quarry Garage HD3 3XJ
   Tel: 01484 654577
   A640 Huddersfield, on left

2. Salendine Shopping Centre HD3 3XA
   Tel: 01484 642355
   A640 Huddersfield, on left

3. Merrie England Coffee Bar HD3 4BU
   Tel: 01484 642820
   A640 Huddersfield, on left

162 Jn 24

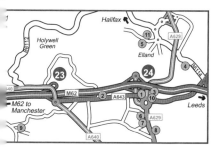

Cedar Court Hotel HD3 3RH
Tel: 01422 375431
At r'bout take Rochdale exit, on right

Nappy Spring Inn & Bistro HD3 3TD
Tel: 01422 372324
A643 Holywell Green, on right

Premier Lodge & Country Carvery HD2 2EA
Tel: 0870 9906488
A643 Brighouse, first left, on right at end of road

The Pinfold B & B HX5 9JU
Tel: 01422 372645
A643 Brighouse, left at lights, on left

5. THE WELLINGTON QUALITY PUB HX5 0DQ
Tel: 01422 372258
Fresh prep. home cooked food every day
Exit to Halifax, follow signs to centre of Elland ♿

6. DE SANDRO PIZZERIA RISTORANTE HD3 3NT
Tel: 01484 512845
Renowned Italian restaurant in Yorkshire
A629 Huddersfield, on right

7. BRIAR COURT HOTEL HD3 3NT
Tel: 01484 519902
48 e/s beds/conf. & function facilities
A629 Huddersfield, on right

8. BP Petrol Station HD3 3
A629 Huddersfield, on left

9. PENNINE MANOR HOTEL & RESTAURANT

Tel: 01484 642368 **HD7 4NH**
Ideally placed for
business/pleasure
A640 R/dale, through Outlane, first left

10. Ainley Top Brewsters HD2 2LB
Tel: 01422 374360
At r'bout South of junction

11. Elland Tyres & Exhausts HX5 9DL
Tel: 01422 375917
A629 North, left to Elland, Providence St

162 Jn 25

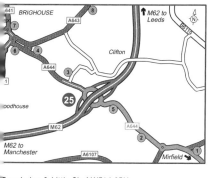

Travelodge & Little Chef WF14 0BY
Tel: 0870 1911646
A644 Mirfield, left to A62, on right

Cooper Bridge Garage WF14 0BU
Tel: 01924 493032
A644 Mirfield, on right

Holiday Inn HD6 4HW
Tel: 0870 4009013
A644 Brighouse, right to Holiday Inn

Robin Hood Garage
Tel: 01484 720504
A644 Brighouse, on right

5. PREMIER LODGE, CHEF & BREWER
PREMIER Tel: 01484 402161
LODGE.com Food served daily
Coaches welcome/CCTV
A644 Mirfield, on right

6. Golden Sea Chinese Restaurant HD6 1PD
Tel: 01484 715554
A644 Brighouse, on left

7. Tesco Supermarket HD6 1RZ
Tel: 0845 6779786
A644 Brighouse, A641 Bradford, on right

8. WILLOW VALLEY GOLF & COUNTRY CLUB

Tel: 01274 878624 **HD6 4JB**
Pay & play golf course
D.range & rest.
A644 Brighouse, right at r'bout, on right

9. WATERFRONT LODGE AND PREGO REST
Tel: 01484 715566 **HD6 1JZ**
Modern hotel and quality Italian rest.
A644 Brighouse, left at lights, through r'bout

M62 Jn 26

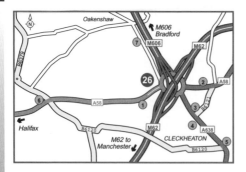

1. Travel Inn & Brewers Fayre BD19 6HG
Tel: 08701 977037
A58 West, on left

2. MID Motor Company Garage BD19 4DN
Tel: 01274 869739
A58 East, on left

3. The Food Bar BD19 4EJ
Tel: 01274 864614
A638 South, on left

4. The Horncastle Inn BD19 3TT
Tel: 01274 869507
A638 South, on right

5. Aakash Restaurant BD19 3PN
A638 South, on left

6. Esso Petrol Station BD12 9
A58 West, on right

7. Richardson Arms BD12 7EN
Tel: 01274 675722
Low Moor exit, on right after Church

M62 Jn 27

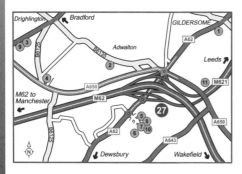

1. THE MILL HOUSE LS27 7LL
Tel: 01132 383810
Excellent food,
friendly, kids welcome
A62 Leeds, on right

2. The Old Brickworks Inn BD11 1EA
Tel: 01132 879132
B6135 Drighlington, on left

3. McFadden's Garage BD11 1AT
Tel: 01132 853996
A650 Bradford, right at r'bout, on right

4. The Mullions Hotel BD11 1JH
Tel: 01132 852451
A650 Bradford, 2nd right, on right

5. Pizza Hut Restaurant WF17 9TB
Tel: 01924 420460
A62 South, left at r'bout

6. **MCDONALD'S RESTAURANT
WF17 9TB**
Tel: 01924 422024
A62 South, on left

7. Frankie & Benny's Restaurant WF17 9TB
Tel: 01924 423767
A62 South, left at r'bout

8. Chiquitos Restaurant WF17 9TB
Tel: 01924 359292
A62 South, left at r'bout

9. Dolphin's Fish & Chips BD11 1BH
Tel: 01132 854284
A650 Bradford, right at r'bout, on right

10. Showcase Cinema Club WF17 9RQ
Tel: 01924 420071
A62 South, left at r'bout

11. Morrisons Store LS27 7JQ
Tel: 01132 527227
Take A650 East, left Nepshaw La

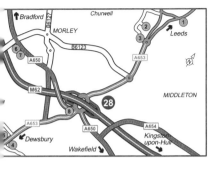

4. Heybeck Petrol Station WF12 7RB
Tel: 01924 472660
A653 Dewsbury, on left

5. Woodkirk Petrol Station WF12 7JB
Tel: 01924 444655
A653 Dewsbury, on right

6. Mermaid Fish Restaurant LS27 0AR
Tel: 0113 2535376
A650 Bradford, on left

Waincliffe Garage LS11 5DA
Tel: 01132 700458
A653 Leeds, on right

White Rose Shopping Centre LS11 8LU
Tel: 01132 291234
A653 Leeds, left at 2nd r'bout

BP Petrol Station LS27 8PU
Tel: 01132 525997
A653 Leeds, left at 2nd r'bout

7. **ASDA SUPERMARKET LS27 0BP**
Tel: 0113 2537518
A650 Bradford, on left

8. THE WHITE BEAR PUB & RESTAURANT
Tel: 0113 253278   **WF3 1JX**
Good food, family pub,
garden & parking
A650 Bradford, on left
HGV

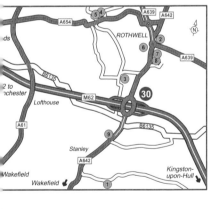

3. New Royds Green Garden Centre LS26 8HB
Tel: 01132 934194
A642 North, 1st left, on left

4. Peggoty's Fine Fish & Chips LS26 0AW
Tel: 01132 826151
A642 North, left at 2 r'bout's, on right

5. Morrisons Supermarket LS26 0QD
Tel: 01132 824248
A642 North, left at 2 r'bout's, on right

6. De Vere Oulton Hall Hotel & Golf Course
Tel: 01132 821000   LS26 8HN
A642 North, left at r'bout

7. Fox & Goose Public House LS26 8EL
Tel: 01132 820202
A642 North, on right

8. The Flower Cabin LS26 8EL
Tel: 01226 295693
A642 North, on right

9. Spindle Tree Public House WF3 4AJ
Tel: 01924 824810
A642 Wakefield, on right

FROBISHER SUITE BAR & RESTAURANT
Tel: 01924 290596   **WF3 4LT**
Canal rest/bar with
exclnt corp. facility
A642 Wakefield, left, on right

Express Holiday Inn LS26 8EJ
Tel: 01132 826201
A642 North, on right after r'bout

M62 Jn 31

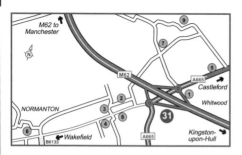

1. TRADING POST PUB & RESTAURANT
Tel: 01977 519587 **WF10 5PE**
Good food in friendly atmos. - play area
A655 Castleford, on right

2. Spices Take-Away WF6 1QU
Tel: 01924 892208
West on Castleford Road, on right

3. Texaco Petrol Station WF6
Tel: 01924 895840
West on Castleford Road, on right

4. **SANDPIPER GUEST HOUSE & CAFÉ WF6 1PY**
Tel: 01924 893122
Small & friendly guest house
West on Castleford Road, on left

5. RISING SUN PUB & QUALITY RESTAURANT
Tel: 01977 554766 **WF10 5PT**
Finest freshly prepared food every day
A655 Castleford, on left

6. W.B. Motors WF6 2DE
Tel: 01924 892154
West on Castleford Road, on right

7. WHITWOOD TRUCK STOP LTD WF10 5QH
Tel: 01977 517690
www.whitwoodtruckstop.co.uk
Follow signs Wakefield Europort

8. New Wheatsheaf Public House WF10 5PZ
Tel: 01977 553052
A655 Castleford, 1st exit at r'bout, 3rd right

9. THE VILLAGE PUB, REST. & MOTEL
Tel: 01924 897171 **WF6 1QY**
40 e/s rooms/conf. & mtg rooms/live ent.
West on Castleford Road, on left

M62 Jn 32

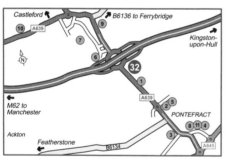

1. The Parkside Hotel WF8 4QD
Tel: 01977 709911
A639 Pontefract, on left

2. MCDONALD'S RESTAURANT WF8 4PR
Tel: 01977 602919
A639 Pontefract, on left after r'bout

3. Queens Hotel/Café Anglais WF8 4DB
Tel: 01977 702228
A639 Pontefract, on right after r'bout

4. Tesco Supermarket WF8 1BJ
Tel: 0845 6779540
A639 Pontefract, on left after r'bout

5. halfords HALFORDS WF8 4PR
Tel: 01977 602966
A639 Pontefract, on left after r'bout

6. Pizza Hut Restaurant WF10 4TA
Tel: 01977 520333
A639 Castleford, first left

7. FREEPORT CASTLEFORD DESIGNER OUTLET
Tel: 01977 520153 **WF10 4SB**
Over 80 shops/open 7 days/free parking
A639 Nth, signposted F/port

8. Hi-Q Tyres & Exhausts WF8 4PQ
Tel: 01977 795353
A639 Pontefract, on left after r'bout

9. BP Petrol Station WF10 4RS
Tel: 01977 553489
A639 Castleford, on right

10. ASDA ASDA SUPERMARKET WF10 5EL
Tel: 01977 512587
A639 Castleford, on right

11. Morrisons Supermarket WF8 4PQ
Tel: 01977 600808
A639 Pontefract, on left

62 Jn 33

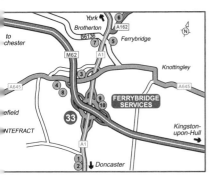

The Darrington Hotel WF8 3BL
Tel: 01977 791458
A1 Darrington, 2nd slip road to Darrington

CHESTNUT HOUSE HOTEL & REST.
Tel: 01977 600046   **WF8 3HR**
Fri evening steak offer - free starters
A1 South, 2nd slip road to Darrington

Travel Inn & Brewsters WF11 0BU
Tel: 08701 977209
A1 Ferrybridge, A645 Pontefract, on right

4. Reg Greenwood Tyres/Exhausts WF8 2LB
   Tel: 01977 702317
   A1 Ferrybridge, A645 Pontefract, on left

5. **GOLDEN LION HOTEL/RIVERSIDE REST.**
   Tel: 01977 673527   **WF11 8ND**
   Food served 7 days, carvery & bar meals
   A1 Ferrybridge, Ferrybridge exit, right under flyover

6. The Brotherton Fox Public House WF11 9EE
   Tel: 01977 672131
   A1 Ferrybridge, Burton Salmon Exit, on left

7. Thorpe Bros Garage WF11 8NN
   Tel: 01977 674561
   A1 Ferrybridge, 2nd exit, on left

8. Texaco Petrol Station WF11
   Tel: 01977 636600
   A1 Ferrybridge, A645 Pontefract, on left

9. S & H Breakdown Recovery Service WF11 0AF
   Tel: 01977 676772
   Situated at junction

10. Travelodge WF11 0AF
    Tel: 0870 1911669
    Situated at junction

62 Jn 34

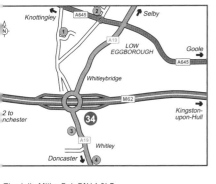

The Jolly Miller Pub DN14 0LB
Tel: 01977 661348
Selby Road, on right

The Horse & Jockey Pub Restaurant DN14 0RX
Tel: 01977 661295
A19 Low Egg., left at crossroads, on right

3. **GEORGE & DRAGON PUBLIC HOUSE DN14 0HY**
   Tel: 01977 661319
   A19 Whitley, on right

4. Whitley Bridge Service Centre DN14 0JB
   Tel: 01977 663040
   A19 Whitley, on left

M62 Jn 36

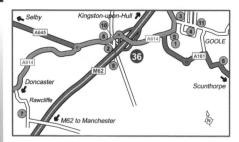

1. GOOLE GAS & WELDING SUPPLIES DN14 6UD
Tel: 01405 762511
Sale of LPG propane ind. gas & equip.
A614 Goole, right at lights, on left

2. Shell Petrol Station DN14 8JS
Tel: 01405 764525
A614 Rawcliffe, on left

3. Clifton Hotel DN14 6AL
Tel: 01405 761336
A614 Goole, right to Boothferry Road, on left

4. *Kwik-Fit* **KWIK-FIT DN14 6AG**
Tel: 01405 780260
A614 Goole, right to Boothferry Road, on right

5. Rapid Fit Tyres/Exhausts DN14 6UA
Tel: 01405 765100
A614 Goole, right at lights, on left

6. Waterways Museum and Adventure Centre DN14 5T
Tel: 01405 768730
A614 Goole, follow signs to Dutch River Side

7. Dominic's Villa Italian Restaurant DN14 8QS
Tel: 01405 831100
A614 Rawcliffe, left to station road, on right

8. Woodside Café (Truckers) DN14 8JU
Tel: 01405 839478
A614 Rawcliffe, on right

9.  **MCDONALD'S RESTAURANT DN14 8JQ**
Tel: 01405 766747
A614 Rawcliffe, on left

10. Travel Inn & Brewers Fayre DN14 8JS
Tel: 01405 722660
A614 Rawcliffe, on left

11. Tesco Supermarket DN14 6BB
Tel: 0845 6779312
A614 Goole, right to Boothferry Road, on left

M62 Jn 37

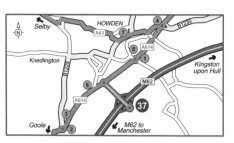

1. BP Petrol Station DN14 7TA
Tel: 01430 430717
A614 Howden, on right

2. Ferryboat Inn DN14 7ED
Tel: 01430 430300
A614 Goole, on left

3. REDBECK MOTEL & AL'S CAFE DN14 7EF
Tel: 01430 430409
A614 Goole, on right

4. Hi-Q Tyres & Exhausts DN14 7AU
Tel: 01430 430464
A614 Howden, on left after 2nd r'bout

5. Wheatsheaf Inn DN14 7SX
Tel: 01430 432334
A614 Howden, left at 2nd r'bout, on right

6. Junction 37 Petrol Station DN14 7DZ
Tel: 01430 430388
A614 Goole, on right

7. The Wellington Hotel DN14 7AE
Tel: 01430 430805
A614 Howden, left to A63, on right

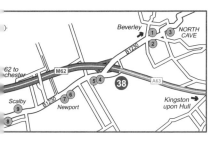

Beverley
NORTH CAVE
62 to chester
Scalby
Newport
Kingston upon Hull

Bridge Garage HU15 2NJ
B1230 North Cave, on left

White Hart Public House & Food HU15 2NJ
Tel: 01430 422432
B1230 North Cave, on right

The Black Swan Pub HU15 2LJ
Tel: 01430 422773
B1230 North Cave, on right

Triangle Motor Co HU15 2RD
Tel: 01430 425038
B1230 Newport, on left

5. Newport Caravans
Tel: 01430 441133
B1230 Newport, on left

6. Johnny Haddock's Quality Fish & Chips HU15 2RG
Tel: 01430 441480
B1230 Newport, on left

7. Asham Balti House Indian Restaurant HU15 2RG
Tel: 01430 449289
B1230 Newport, on left

8. The Yorkshire Garden Centre HU15 2UJ
Tel: 01430 440169
B1230 Newport, left to Tongue Lane, 1st right

9. The White Horse Hotel HU15 2UP
Tel: 01430 440269
B1230 Newport, on right

10. Wards Hotel HU15 2SL
Tel: 01430 440356
B1230 Newport, left to Tongue Lane, 1st right

FREE Freshly Ground Coffee with any Toasted Bagel or portion of Fruit Toast™ purchased

i'm lovin' it

Valid before 10.30am until 31/12/05.

Valid at participating McDonald's Restaurants.

BEANS SELECTED BY

Buy any Extra Value Meal* and get one FREE

i'm lovin' it

Valid after 10.30am until 31/12/05.

Valid at participating McDonald's Restaurants.